YOU CAN'T LIBEL THE DEAD

A life in journalism

YOU CAN'T LIBEL THE DEAD

A life in journalism

Neil Benson

This edition published 2021 by:
Takahe Publishing Ltd.
Registered Office:
77 Earlsdon Street, Coventry CV5 6EL

Copyright © Neil Benson 2021

ISBN 978-1-908837-22-6

TAKAHE PUBLISHING LTD. 2021

For my wife Jo and our children Joe, Rory and Meredith. All the stories I've bored you with over the years, now in one handy package.

Contents

Contents

PREFACE

Soon after starting my first job as a know-nothing 19-year-old trainee reporter, one of my more seasoned colleagues decided to share the benefit of his wisdom. "The pay's crap," he told me. "But you'll have a few laughs." He was right on both counts.

Journalism has always attracted an endless flow of eager youngsters, desperate to chase their dream. So the law of supply and demand dictates that the starting pay will never be great.

By way of illustration, I started my first job in journalism on my hometown paper, *The Star*, in Sheffield, on July 22, 1974, at a salary of just over £24 a week – a fiver less than I'd earned a year earlier as a council binman. So, kids, if money is what gets you out of bed in the morning, forget journalism and try merchant banking.

But unlike the vast majority of jobs, life as a journalist, as my old colleague said, is frequently funny. Funny as in strange. And funny as in … really, really funny.

In this memoir, I'll share a selection of my "war stories" and introduce you to some of the characters I've had the pleasure of meeting in my 45 years in the news industry. They are a colourful bunch, and I hope I've done them justice. I witnessed or was personally involved in the vast majority of these tales, so I can vouch for the overall veracity, if not for every detail. A few stories are second or third hand, some have been handed down as part of office folklore, and one is certainly apocryphal but I've included it purely for comedy value. There's also a splash of thinly-researched social history here and there.

This book covers the first two-thirds of my career, spent in regional and national newspaper newsrooms. In the final third, as editorial director of Trinity Mirror's regional business, a large chunk of my time was spent at the corporate HQ, where life was a little more strait-laced.

My job took me to the sharp end of some landmark news stories, including a notorious mass murder, the Bradford City Fire and the unmasking of a much-loved parish priest as a serial paedophile. And there was a memorable day when an armed robber turned up at the office, wanting to see me. I've described these events at greater length, from my perspective as a journalist and editor.

Journalism can be a doorway to many worlds. My career took me to newspapers in Sheffield, Manchester, Bradford (twice), Northampton, Coventry, Newcastle and Teesside, before spending 16 itinerant years as editorial director, working with editors across the UK. I was exceptionally fortunate that my job also took me to the USA, Hong Kong, Pakistan, South Africa and most of Western Europe.

I've driven a drugs-busting police boat, been 3,000 feet up in an Army helicopter and 1,500 feet underground in a coal mine. I've seen the inside of 10 Downing Street, Buckingham Palace and a Peshawar jail, and I've met people from every part of the social spectrum – from millionaire sports stars to those in abject poverty, from criminals and their victims to Prime Ministers and the Royal Family. I have journalism to thank for that.

In relating these memories, I also wanted to share some thoughts about the seismic changes that have shaken the news industry during my working lifetime. While the fun by no means stopped, I'd have to admit that life became considerably more serious as the industry fought – and continues to fight – for its life.

Along the way, I encountered many first-class journalists. One of the best was the late Bob James: newspaper production guru, author, master of typography and doyen of journalism trainers. Among many other things, Bob taught hundreds of journalists about life as an editor, how to be a better training manager and the practical side of newspaper law. A pearl of his wisdom that doesn't appear in the textbooks was: "If you're going to libel a police officer, make sure it's a superintendent, not a PC. The same goes for schools. You're better off libelling a head than a teacher."

Bob knew that, thanks to its large membership, the Police Federation had huge reserves of cash and was therefore much more likely to pursue you in the courts than the smaller and much more modestly-funded Superintendents' Association. The same applied to the National Union of Teachers versus the headteachers' union, the NAHT. As I discovered later, he might usefully have added: "Beware millionaires who own football clubs."

I've never kept a diary. The anecdotes that follow are written from memory, with a little help from my friends, family, former colleagues, Dr Google and

Preface

Professor Wikipedia. Where names have been omitted, it is either to protect the innocent or to help me dodge a potential libel bullet.

And on that score, Bob James had another, more encouraging, piece of advice. "The good news," he said, "is that you can't libel the dead."

Chapter One

Bloodstains in the Snow

I t was around 1 o'clock in the morning when I stumbled downstairs to answer the phone, half asleep and half cut, after a few Friday night pints with my dad. News editor David Mastin apologised for getting me out of bed. It might be something or nothing, he said, but one of our photographers had called in to say he had been driving home from a night out when he spotted a big police presence outside The Highwayman pub, high on the moors between Chesterfield and Baslow. Could I nip out there and take a look? And, by the way, are you OK to drive? I answered yes to both questions.

Recently qualified as a senior reporter on my hometown paper, *The Star*, in Sheffield, I was pleased that, from a pool of around 20 reporters, it was me that Mastin had called. Or maybe his first choices just decided to let the phone ring. No matter. On a bitterly cold January night, I pulled on my duffle coat and scarf, jumped into my VW Beetle and headed for the hills.

When I pulled into The Highwayman car park an hour later, a blizzard was raging. There were arc lights and a police mobile incident room in the pub car park – sure signs that something big was going on. Two journalists had got there before me: Martyn Sharpe, of *The Sun*, and the *Daily Express's* legendary North of England reporter Peggy Robinson. I knew both of them by reputation. Neither of them knew me from Adam. We chatted guardedly for a few minutes, trying to glean snippets of information from each other. The two experienced national reporters were giving nothing away, and I had nothing to give.

Then Derbyshire's assistant chief constable stepped out of the incident room. A man of his rank on top of the moors, in a blizzard, in the early hours, on a Saturday? Another sign that something big was happening. He walked over to us but, apart from a few pleasantries, he wasn't saying much either.

After a minute or two of awkward small talk, Robinson asked how 'Mrs Maron" was. The ACC corrected her – the name was Moran, and he spelled it out. The three of us scribbled it into our notebooks. A bit more sparring and then Robinson asked, casually: 'How many bodies are there?' Yes, this was definitely big.

From an early age, Billy Hughes was trouble. At school, anti-social behaviour and petty crimes escalated quickly into more serious offences. He spent time in approved school and Borstal before being sentenced, at the age of 20, to his first spell in prison. Preston-born Hughes had married and fathered a child but the relationship was scarred by his violence. In 1976, he left his wife and moved to Chesterfield. Five months later, on an August night, he followed a young couple he had met in a nightclub and, as they walked home through a park, Hughes smashed the man over the head with a brick and raped his girlfriend.

There was widespread media coverage of the attack and, following a tip-off, police arrested Hughes. He was charged with rape and grievous bodily harm, and remanded to Leicester Prison, to be brought back to Chesterfield each week for further remand by the town's magistrates until he could be sent for trial at the Crown Court.

On several occasions, I was in court to report on the brief remand hearing. Hughes, aged 30, was dark-haired, short and wiry. Considering the seriousness of the charges he was facing, he looked remarkably relaxed and wore a constant half-smile. It was on the way to one of these routine court appearances that he made a daring and bloody escape.

The prison authorities, who had not been given details of Hughes' previous convictions for violence, had put him to work in the kitchen, from where he stole a knife. On the way to Chesterfield by taxi, in handcuffs and escorted by two prison officers, he asked to stop at a service station to use the lavatory. While alone and uncuffed, he retrieved the hidden knife and, as he got back into the taxi, stabbed both officers in the neck, injuring them seriously. After forcing the taxi driver to continue for a short distance, Hughes then dumped him and the prison officers at the side of the road.

Hughes drove off but after a short distance he crashed the car. He then fled on foot. Over the following days, the local papers and broadcast news bulletins were headlining on the hunt for the dangerous fugitive as the worst blizzards for 15 years swept across the Derbyshire moors.

* * * *

Richard and Gill Moran lived with their ten-year-old adopted daughter Sarah and Gill's retired parents, Arthur and Amy Minton. The family had converted an old pottery barn at Eastmoor, a remote hamlet on the edge of the Peak District National Park, and renamed it Pottery Cottage.

Richard, a sales director, and Gill, a secretary at an accountancy firm, are at work when Billy Hughes walks into their home, cold, wet and exhausted, carrying two axes he had found in their garden shed. It is Wednesday lunchtime.

He tells the Mintons he is on the run, and that he needs to lay low until nightfall. He says he won't harm them. Later that afternoon, Gill and Sarah arrive home to be confronted by Hughes. Gill attempts to keep her young daughter calm by telling her he is a stranded motorist. The girl sits on the floor while the adults drink coffee and talk. Gill would later tell police that Hughes' manner was friendly at first but as they waited for her husband Richard to return from work, he grew agitated.

Richard arrives home to find Hughes holding a knife to Gill's throat. Hughes binds and gags him before tying up Gill and her mother. He then carries them upstairs and puts them in separate rooms. He ties up Arthur in an armchair.

On Thursday morning, a workman arrives at the cottage to empty the septic tank. Believing their best hope of survival is to do as Hughes says, Gill tries to remain calm as she signs a docket to confirm the work has been done. She glimpses her father in the armchair, covered by a coat. Hughes tells her he is sleeping. Later, she notices he is no longer in the chair.

Hughes forces the Morans to phone their workplaces and Sarah's school to say they are all sick. He sends Gill to Chesterfield to buy cigarettes and a newspaper, with the threat that he will harm her family if she does 'anything silly'. A few hours later, after Gill has returned and made soup and toast, Hughes and his captives read the papers and play cards.

On Friday morning, Hughes gives Gill and Richard a shopping list – tinned food, cigarettes, sweets, a camping stove and a gas cylinder – and sends them to Chesterfield. He gives Gill £25 he has found in the house and tells them to 'buy a nice present for Sarah'. The couple do the shopping and buy Sarah an Enid Blyton book. They also buy a newspaper, which has Hughes' picture on the front page.

When the couple arrive home, Hughes demands they take him to Richard's office, to search for cash. They find a couple of hundred pounds. When they arrive back at Pottery Cottage, he ties up Richard and loads his supplies into the car. He drives off with Gill but they turn back when Hughes says he has forgotten a road atlas. He tells Gill to wait outside, saying: 'I'm just going to check on Sarah and your dad.'

When he returns, the car won't start and a furious Hughes orders Gill to get help. As Hughes tries to coax the engine into life, she whispers to her neighbours, the Newmans, that Richard is tied up. As Gill gets back into the car, her mother Amy appears, staggering in the road, her throat cut. She falls to the snow-covered ground in a pool of blood. Hughes drags her body back to the cottage. When he returns, he hears a car start – the Newmans, who don't have a phone, are driving off to alert the police.

Hughes knocks at another door and asks mechanic Ron Frost for a tow, to get the car going. Gill mouths a few words to Frost's wife Madge. Frost manages to start the car and Hughes drives off with Gill as his hostage. By the time Frost gets back home, at around 8.20pm, his wife has alerted the police.

Officers arrive at Pottery Cottage to find Richard, Sarah, Amy and Arthur dead. Meanwhile, the Morans' Chrysler is being driven by Hughes at breakneck speed over the Cat & Fiddle Road between Derbyshire and Cheshire, tailed by an unmarked police car. When the police pull in front of them, the Chrysler crashes into a wall. As two officers approach the car, Hughes holds an axe above Gill's head, shouting: 'Back off or I'll kill her.' He drags Gill out of the car and demands the officers give him the keys to their vehicle. As Hughes drives the hijacked Morris Marina towards Cheshire, police marksmen are flooding into the area.

By 10pm, the police have positioned a bus to block the A5002, near the village of Rainow. Hughes attempts to swerve around it but crashes into a dry-stone wall. Armed officers swarm around the Marina but can't shoot, for fear of hitting Gill. Hughes demands another car, to make his getaway. Negotiators talk to him for 50 minutes and think they may be calming him when he suddenly screams: 'Your time's up' and he raises the axe to strike Gill.

Chief Inspector Peter Howse, the man leading the hunt, hurls himself through the broken window of the car, thudding into Hughes just as he brings down the axe. It skims Gill's head and falls on to the rear seat. As Howse grapples with the killer, a marksman shoots but the bullet glances off Hughes's head, making him even wilder. A second police marksman takes aim. Three more shots ring out. The final bullet penetrates his heart, and Hughes is dead.

Gill, injured by Hughes' axe and flying glass, is taken to hospital. Later, a detective breaks the news that her husband, daughter, mother and father have all been murdered. Hughes had stabbed them multiple times in the throat and chest. The police found Richard, Sarah and Arthur's bodies inside the house. Amy's body was in the garden, where she had been dumped by Hughes, partially covered by snow. When Hughes said Arthur was asleep in the armchair, he was already dead. He killed ten-year-old Sarah while Gill was in Chesterfield, buying newspapers, cigarettes and the Enid Blyton book. Richard and Amy had their throats cut when Hughes returned to the house 'to look after Sarah and your dad'.

* * * *

By 5 o'clock on that shudderingly-cold January morning, I was in *The Star*'s Chesterfield office, sitting at a typewriter and puzzling how to begin to tell this monumental story. The phone rang – it was deputy news editor Alan Powell, asking if I could use some help. I certainly could. Within half an hour he was sitting beside me and together we wrote the splash for Saturday's edition.

Some of the detail I've described emerged over the next few days but the main thread of the story – the cold-blooded murders, the car chases, the axe held above Gill Moran's head and the shooting of Hughes – had been confirmed by the police overnight. Because the drama had unfolded just hours before, in pitch darkness, there were no news pictures to illustrate my story. So the news desk commissioned an artist's impression for Page One, showing a police marksman firing into the car as Hughes held the axe above Gill Moran's head.

With the splash written, I spent the rest of the morning seeking out other angles for a special edition *The Star* had decided to publish. The local radio stations' news bulletins acted as a billboard for our more detailed coverage and papers were flying off the newsagents' shelves.

I visited an address in Chesterfield where Hughes had been staying before his arrest and door-knocked his landlord, a former soldier, who described living with Hughes. In truth, he didn't have much of interest to say. I kept going for another few hours, working on follow-ups for Monday's edition, but by mid-afternoon the adrenaline ran out. Lack of sleep began to catch up with me and I headed for home.

There was blanket coverage of the murders in the next day's national Sundays, many of them focusing on Hughes's long record of violence. The most gruesome anecdote was in the *Sunday Times*, who unearthed a story about one of Hughes's arrests some years earlier. He was so violent that a posse of police officers struggled to control him. Eventually they managed to bundle him into the back of a large police van. Then they threw in a police Alsatian and shut the doors, believing that being confronted by a large, snarling dog would subdue him. After a few seconds, there was a yelp, then silence. They opened the doors to find the dog dead. Hughes had wrenched its front legs apart and burst its heart.

One week after the dramatic conclusion to Hughes' killing spree, I was sent to Brimington Cemetery, in Chesterfield, to cover the funerals of the Moran family. Martyn Sharpe, who I'd met on that freezing night in The Highwayman car park, was there for *The Sun*. As we stood on the roadside outside the cemetery, he paid me a small compliment on the work I'd done the previous week. The world's print and broadcast media were out in force but the police ensured there was little for us to see or to report on. The funeral car carrying Gill Moran was switched en route to the cemetery and arrived with a police escort, to keep reporters at arm's length.

The Home Office, who were responsible for Hughes' funeral, had arranged for him to be buried at Boythorpe, on the other side of Chesterfield, four days later. A grave had been prepared but there was an enforced change of plan after protests by locals, furious that the killer's burial there would be a permanent reminder of his awful crimes. Instead, he was cremated at Brimington Cemetery, where his victims are buried.

All the national papers wanted the first-hand story of Gill Moran's terrible ordeal. She agreed to talk to the *Daily Mail*, who were reputed to have paid £60,000 – a phenomenal sum at the time – for world exclusive rights. As she interviewed Mrs Moran for the *Mail*'s eight-part serialisation, Lynda Lee-Potter observed: "Gill wept convulsively with her arms tightly wrapped round her body, swaying backwards and forwards. Horror and grief annihilated her."

Five years later, Yorkshire TV revealed plans for a dramatisation of the Pottery Cottage Murders but the project was scrapped following an outcry by local people. The memory was still too raw.

As Lee-Potter described, three days at the hands of a cold-blooded psychopath had left indelible marks on Gill Moran. But she bravely rebuilt her life, remarrying and moving to Ireland with her new husband. She has never spoken to the media again.

That bleak night in January 1977 was a landmark in the lives of others, too.

Alan Nicholls, the policeman who fired the final, fatal shot, was the first officer from the Derbyshire force to shoot anyone dead. It was also the first time British police had shot dead an escaped prisoner. In 2017, eight years after his death, Nicholls' colleagues commemorated his bravery with a plaque in his honour.

Chief Inspector Peter Howse, who grappled with Hughes in order to save Gill Moran's life, revealed in 2020 that the killings still haunted him, more than four decades later.

And, at the age of 22, I had covered the biggest story of my reporting life.

Chapter Two

You Had Me at 'Bludgeoned'

If anyone tells you there was nothing to do during the Great Covid Lockdown, have them beamed back to any random Sunday in 1963, for a taste of true misery. Every shop closed. A grand total of two TV channels – both in fuzzy black and white, and neither of them showing football. In fact, there was no sport at all on Sunday, unless you count Ski Sunday, which of course you can't. If Childline had existed, I'd have called them. Only we didn't have a phone.

As a child growing up in the early Sixties, I hated Sundays. No offence, Sunday, but in the eyes of an energetic nine-year-old you were dull. Let me rephrase that. You were crushingly, mind-bendingly, life-sappingly, endlessly boring. Saturday, on the other hand, was the dog's doodahs of a day. And the two Saturdays a month I spent with my grandparents, Joe and Kitty, were the best of all.

I was born at my grandparents' old house – 169 South Street – just behind Sheffield Midland Station, in the city's Park district. This seems a curious name for an area of decaying housing with shared outdoor privies and without, so far as I am able to ascertain, the merest hint of a park. When my parents wed, they moved in with Joe, Kitty and their lodger, and remained there for the first four years of their married life. This wasn't a lifestyle choice. It was forced on them by a combination of dereliction and Hitler's bombs, which claimed the lives of 700 Sheffielders and damaged 82,000 homes – half the city's housing stock.

It must have been a squeeze in No. 169, particularly after I and my sister Karen came along. But in the spring of 1957, with the Park district slums finally scheduled for demolition, we and most of our close relatives were rehoused on Sheffield's newest and biggest council estate, Gleadless Valley. My parents finally had their first home together – three bedrooms, indoor loo, garden front and back, and a brick-built outhouse. 'LUXURY!' as Monty Python's Four Yorkshiremen would say. Joe and Kitty were rehomed just round the corner, and my mum's parents, two of her sisters and two brothers were all within a spit.

Nowadays, Gleadless Valley doesn't have the best reputation. On a visit to Sheffield, my son mentioned to a guy in a pub that I was from 'The Valley', which prompted the reply: "Bloody hell, don't forget your stab vest." You get the drift.

But, back in the day, being allocated a council house on The Valley was like winning the pools. Everything – the houses, the shops, the schools – was brand, spanking new, and there was green space everywhere. The estate, which houses more than 20,000 people, was designed by Sheffield's City Architect J. Lewis Womersley. His most celebrated project is the Park Hill flats development, a brutalist monolith with a somewhat chequered history. Over the years, it has undergone several reinventions, first as the athletes' accommodation for the 1991 World Student Games, then as university flats and most recently as private apartments. But, as the Municipal Dreams blog points out, Womersley's "supreme, but often overlooked, achievement is the Gleadless Valley estate, which combined urban housing types and the natural landscape so effectively that it still looks stunning, especially on a bright winter's day."

When we moved in, I was two and Karen just six weeks old. My youngest sister, Diane, was born in the new house a couple of years later, completing my parents' contribution to the post-war Baby Boom. Many of the fresh-as-paint houses and maisonettes were home to young families, which meant there were always plenty of potential playmates around. When we reached junior school age, summer evenings were filled with hours-long street football matches or games of hide-and-seek in the wood that ran through the estate. Growing up there felt utterly safe. Except, perhaps, for that time a young woman from across the road battered her father to death with a vice. More on that later.

My grandad Joe, silver hair Brylcreemed back, was tall and slim. He had had a variety of jobs – driving lorries, fitting carpets and, most recently, in the steel works. He was my hero. Joe didn't like signs of weakness, which, in the end, was his undoing. Recovering from a serious heart attack, he went against medical advice by insisting on walking to the local barber's rather than catch a bus for a piffling two stops. After around 250 paces, while passing the local primary school where my sisters were learning their times tables, 66-year-old Joe dropped to the pavement, dead. He really should have listened to the doctor.

Joe was one of three brothers. Bill, who owned a carpet shop, had done the best for himself financially. The other brother was Horace, who, with his wife Lizzie, ran The New Inn, on Duke Street, a short step from the house where I was born.

As was the tradition in South Yorkshire, every Whit Sunday my parents would take me and my two sisters, wearing a new suit of clothes, to see our relatives. They would pat us on the head, tell us how smart we looked and give us a coin or two.

On this most exciting of days, the visit to The New Inn was always the high point, partly because it was the furthest flung family outpost (about three miles distant) but mostly because to reach the living quarters you had to pass through the public bar. It was packed with working-class men in their Sunday-best suits, consuming a generous Bank Holiday ration of Joshua Tetley's bitter and producing so much eye-watering cigarette smoke that visibility was down to a few feet. Exotic? It was off the scale.

Kitty was the brains of the grandparenting outfit. She was small, self-contained, partial to a bottle of Guinness, and opinionated, in a quietly formidable way. My mum would always remind me to behave myself when I went to see her and Joe. She really didn't need to.

Kitty was born Kate Ellen Jordan, in 1899, the second youngest of Walter and Florence Jordan's eight children. Like his father, grandfather and great-grandfather before him, Walter worked in the Sheffield cutlery industry, as an edge tool grinder. Three of his sons followed Walter into this dirty, dangerous job, which required the operator to sit astride a rapidly-revolving grindstone. One of my relatives has a photograph of Walter's father, Bertin, his clothes shredded by a grindstone which split while spinning at high speed. His life was saved by the several layers of thick clothing he was wearing - the 'personal protective equipment' of the time. The main killer of edge tool grinders, though, was not a runaway grindstone but respiratory disease, caused by the dust generated in the grinding process. Bertin and his son Walter were both dead by the age of 50, victims of silicosis. They didn't wear face masks back then.

With ten mouths to feed, money in the Jordan household was extremely tight. Both my grandmothers told me that, to get through the week, their mothers would often have to pawn their children's shoes. I can recall only one occasion when Kitty talked in any depth about her childhood. She was in her 70s but I could sense the underlying anger as she described the hardship her family had faced in the early years of the 20th Century.

Kitty was intensely proud of passing her matriculation and as we talked she reached into a drawer and pulled out her perfectly-kept matriculation booklet, which marked the end of her education, at the age of 12. That same year, her father had died. She was clearly a bright child but, in common with many of her generation and social class, life offered her precious little by way of opportunity.

For my grandparents' generation, who raised their children in the inter-war years, large families were the norm; my mum Vera was one of eight. To be an only child, like my father Eric, was unusual. I suspect this was a conscious choice on Kitty's part, born of a determination that her boy would be dealt a better hand in life.

Joe and Kitty's lodger, Bryce Nicholls, had begun living with them before he headed off to war, where he served in the RAF. On demobilisation, he turned up at their door and resumed his lodgings. When Joe and Kitty moved to Gleadless Valley, Uncle Bryce – my godfather – went with them.

Occasionally, when it was my sisters' turn to spend Saturday with our grandparents, Bryce would take me to Hillsborough, where we would watch Sheffield Wednesday play out a drab, goalless draw. If Wednesday were away from home, he might take me to the cinema. Together, we saw *How the West Was Won* (Answer: By John Wayne, ably supported by a galaxy of Hollywood's finest, with narration by Spencer Tracy). We saw *Ben Hur*, which starred Charlton Heston driving a Roman chariot, and *Summer Holiday*, which starred Cliff Richard driving a London bus.

Whether it was football or a film, my days out with Bryce would end at Mary Gentle's Café, in Howard Street, for fish and chips. No doubt about it, in the Godfather Sweepstake, I drew the golden ticket.

* * * *

My Saturdays with Joe and Kitty ran to a wonderfully predictable pattern. We'd start by catching a bus to 'town' and head for the Castle Market - another J. Lewis Womersley production, built on the ruins of Sheffield Castle. More specifically, we would visit the Fish Market, a name which grossly undersold the array of fish, meat, pies, game, fruit and veg on offer.

Atop every butcher's stall was an upside-down army of dead rabbits, gutted but still in their fur coats, strung from hooks by their back legs, with plastic bags over their heads. I asked Grandad Joe what the bags were for. No, it wasn't a mass suicide pact. He explained that the bags were there to prevent any blood still in their little bodies from dripping on to the white-coated butchers below. Seeing these battalions of dead bunnies always triggered a pang of sadness in me. Fortunately, I'd always managed to shrug it off by the time one of them turned up in a stew a few days later.

Once in the market, there was no browsing. Kitty knew what she wanted and, like a 5ft 0ins, heat-seeking missile, she set about bagging it. If Saturday was to run according to plan, speed at this early stage was of the essence. Shopping done, we'd head for home, with me clutching a mammoth bag of miniature cheese biscuits to sustain me on the half-hour bus journey.

As Kitty made lunch (which we, like all working class Northerners, called dinner), Joe and I headed for the living room to set up for the afternoon. Him in his armchair – an antimacassar in place to ensure the chintz upholstery remained Brylcreem-free – and me lying on the carpet next to the gas fire. He would read the *Daily Mirror* from cover to cover, paying particular attention to the racing pages. His 'investments' decided upon, he would pass the paper to me before nipping across the road to the betting shop. I would have a casual flick through, because I wanted to be like him.

After lunch, it was back to the living room for Joe to conduct the ceremonial closing of the curtains, the better to see the grainy black-and-white picture produced by the TV. A couple of minutes for the tube to warm up and then … here it comes … the theme tune and glorious opening titles of the BBC's flagship live sports show, *Grandstand*.

There followed four hours of the best sport the Beeb had to offer. Back then, they had a monopoly on all the big, annual events – the Grand National, the Boat Race, the FA Cup final, Wimbledon. The content on an average week, though, could be pretty thin gruel but to a sport-starved kid and his grandad, it was a feast.

Horse racing was the cornerstone, introduced by the peerless duo of Clive Graham and Peter O'Sullevan, racing correspondents of the *Daily Express*. Swimming was a regular feature, as was snooker, with commentary by 'Whispering' Ted Lowe, coiner of those timeless lines "For those of you watching in black and white, the pink is next to the green"; and, as former world champion Fred Davis struggled to rest his leg on the rail of the table to take on a long pot: "He's getting on a bit and is having trouble getting his leg over."

Also in the content mix was a pot pourri of minority-interest sports, including showjumping, scrambling, motocross, speedway and hill climbing, all of which required competitors to have access to either a horse or a motor vehicle. As far as participation went, these activities were light years beyond the reach of the millions of ordinary folk who formed the core of *Grandstand*'s audience. But that didn't matter. However obscure the sport, however unfeasibly posh the participants, Joe and I devoured it all.

The living room fog, which had been thickening steadily with each Senior Service the old boy lit up, was disturbed at 4pm sharp, when Kitty entered the sanctum. Without a word, Joe would get out of his chair and switch channels to ITV's *World of Sport* for the wrestling, with our host Kent Walton. After her fix of Jackie Pallo, Mick McManus and Billy Two Rivers, Kitty would decamp to the kitchen again to make our tea. The only known-unknown here was whether it would be finnan haddock or kippers. Or possibly crumpets.

Joe would then flick back to the BBC for the highlight of the day, the football results, brought to us via the cutting-edge technology of the videprinter. This was an oversized typewriter which chugged out the scores while the smartly-suited David Coleman added the contextual detail – "That's eight games without a goal for Sheffield Wednesday" – which brought it to life. Sixty years later, this has evolved into *Gillette Soccer Saturday*, in which smartly-suited men describe in over-excited detail a plethora of live action that we, the viewers, can't see. Then and now, it makes great telly.

Saturdays at Joe and Kitty's had a comforting predictability, like pulling on your favourite old sweater. You knew what to expect, and it was always reassuringly warm and lovely. Those happy days have merged into a single, blurry, childhood memory. Except ...

One Saturday morning, as we waited for Grandstand to start, I picked up Joe's well-thumbed copy of the Mirror. Within seconds, the front-page had me transfixed. The lead story was a report on the trial of a multiple murderer, a topic which might well grab the attention of most young boys. But it wasn't the description of the gory crimes that caught my eye, it was the use of two particular words. Below each head-and-shoulders photograph of the killer's eight victims was a caption, giving the name of each one and describing them as either 'bludgeoned' or 'cudgelled'.

Now, if you put a bludgeon and a cudgel alongside one another, I'm not sure many of us would know the difference. The dictionary defines a bludgeon as: "a thick stick with a heavy end, used as a weapon", whereas a cudgel is: "a short, thick stick, used as a weapon". It's a subtle distinction, to say the least. I wonder if, before setting out on one of his murderous rampages, the killer used to take a moment to ponder whether he should employ the cudgel, or was today more of a bludgeon day?

It's unlikely the *Mirror* sub-editor who wrote those captions was too fussed about the fine detail. But his choice of those two words brought the story home to me in such a graphic way that I couldn't stop reading them, over and over. Bludgeoned. Cudgelled. Bludgeoned. Cudgelled.

If I was to apply a little journalistic licence, I could say this was the moment a small boy knew he was destined to be a newspaperman. But it wasn't. By the time I was 13, I had set my heart on becoming a pathologist. This decision was driven entirely by the popular TV show *The Expert*, starring Marius Goring as Dr John Hardy, who would use his forensic skill and searing powers of deduction to solve a fiendishly tricky case every Sunday night on BBC 1. Sadly, my hopes of a glittering scientific career came crashing down just a few months later, when I received of my end-of-year Chemistry and Biology results.

Over the next few years, other career ideas came and went. It wasn't until I was 18 that I decided for certain that journalism was the job for me. But those two words on the *Daily Mirror* front page ensured that, from the age of nine, I was hooked on the newspaper drug.

Bludgeoned. Cudgelled. Bludgeoned. Cudgelled. It's a close-run thing, but I think 'bludgeoned' is my favourite.

Chapter Three

From 'Boy!' To Man

At the age of 15, I sacrificed my afternoons watching *Grandstand* to start my first job in a newsroom, as a part-time copy boy on *The Star*'s Saturday sports special, the *Green 'Un*. Up and down the country, evening newspapers would put together football editions, almost always on coloured paper. Most were Greens or Pinks. The one exception I know of was the *Yorkshire Sports*, produced by the *Telegraph & Argus*, in Bradford, which was printed on a more muted, buff-coloured paper. Kirsty Allsopp and Phil Spencer would have approved.

Considering the labour-intensive, heavy-industrial method of production, the speed with which sports specials were produced and distributed was mightily impressive. Minutes after the final whistle, the crowds walking away from Hillsborough or Bramall Lane towards Sheffield bus station would be met by news vendors, a bagful of papers slung over their shoulder, shouting "RRRREEEEN 'UN! GET YOURRRRREEEEN 'UN!" The papers would sell quickly and be tucked under the buyer's arm, to be read on the bus, at home or over a pint at the local.

Most of the sports special's content was put together during the week – in the *Green 'Un*'s case by its editor Reg Whitaker. Football was the bedrock, with a comprehensive mix of background pieces on Sheffield United and Sheffield Wednesday, plus the more peripheral clubs in the *Star*'s circulation area, Rotherham United, Barnsley, Chesterfield, Worksop Town and Mansfield. Semi-professional sport was well served, as were the grassroots – reaching as far down as school sport. If it moved and was wearing shorts, the Green 'Un wanted to know about it.

A unique service offered by the *Green 'Un* was to carry school football scores in the front-page results panel. If someone from the school took the trouble to ring in with the score, they were guaranteed to be published. It fell to me, an enthusiastic right back of limited ability, to phone in our result every Saturday lunchtime. Seeing City Grammar U13s 3, Firth Park U13s 1 on the front page, just below the Wednesday and United scores, was a genuine thrill. It was also a smart piece of marketing by the *Green 'Un*, as it ensured that every member of the school squad would buy a copy, to see their result in lights.

Only once did the system fail us. I had phoned in our result as usual but for some reason it didn't appear. At school on Monday morning, my teammates vented their anger, not least because we had recorded a thumping win. Try as I might, I couldn't convince them it was the *Green 'Un*'s fault, not mine. This, I now realise, was my first experience of having to deal with a complaint from an angry reader. There would be plenty more where that came from.

If editor Reg ploughed a lonely furrow on weekdays, when Saturday came he had a phalanx of extra resource at his disposal. As well as a full-strength sports desk, he could call on around ten news sub-editors who transformed into football experts at 3pm, when every match kicked off.

Then there were the copytakers, a bank of middle-aged ladies, each equipped with a typewriter and a set of earphones, who clattered away furiously as the football reporters dictated their copy from the grounds at pre-agreed points through the afternoon. This reporting process, known as a 'runner', involves filing a pre-game piece – the team news, weather and so on – and additional material midway through each half and at half time. On the final whistle, the reporter files the first few paragraphs of their article (the 'nose') summarising the story of the match and the result. The digital revolution has changed many aspects of journalism, but the traditional 'runner' is still used by reporters covering live sport today.

With so many games being reported and with numerous pages to fill in the tightest of time windows, speed was paramount. After every few paragraphs, the copytaker would pull the copy paper from her typewriter and shout: "Boy!". That was the signal for one of us copy-boys to run over, grab the copy and transfer it to the sub-editor handling that match, leaving the copytaker free to continue typing.

With calls coming in thick and fast, often over crackly phone lines with a football crowd providing the backing track, mistakes were bound to happen. For example, when a cricket freelance told a copytaker that a game had been halted because of sea fret, the copy that landed on the subs' desk read: C. Frett stopped play. To be fair to the copytakers, they also saved many a reporter from committing egregious howlers, usually by asking gently: 'Are you sure you mean that?'

The Facebook group Horny Handed Subs of Toil has gathered a fine collection of copytaking bloopers. A few of my favourites: '... then Tony Jacklin took a sandwich (sand wedge) from his bag.'; the scorers for Wales were Russian Jews (Rush and Hughes); and 'An RAF pilot ejaculated over Shropshire'.

For the half-dozen 15- to 18-year-olds in the pool, having to respond to a cry of "Boy!" was slightly demeaning. Particularly so for Pete, the oldest of us, who had Jesus-length hair, a full beard and an achingly cool taste in music. But the extra cash we were earning helped even Pete to get over it.

It was during my time as a copy boy that I spoke to my first real, live journalist – *The Star*'s No. 2 court reporter Ray Linfoot. While the No. 1 guy, Peter Evans, spent most of his time covering the big trials in Sheffield Crown Court, Ray's beat was the magistrates court, where minor cases are heard. As a journalist, he wasn't a high flyer but he was easy-going, with a ready smile, and he would often pop over for a chat with us during his downtime. I would ask him about his job, and he made it sound pretty cool, even though – as I was to discover later – covering magistrates' court is not the most glamorous role in the newsroom.

On Saturdays, after spending the morning writing up pieces for the day's edition, Ray's attention would turn to football. His role was to man the Creed Room, where the half-time and full-time scores from all four English divisions and Scotland would come in on tape. After introducing himself over the Tannoy system with his signature greeting: 'Good afternoon, sports fans!', he would read out the scores.

Two floors below, in the composing room, a handful of men from the accounts department sat at a desk covered in neatly-arranged slips of coloured paper, one for each game being played. As Ray read out the scores, they would fill in the relevant slip and hand it to a copy boy, who would ferry it 20 metres or so to the 'slot', where the results were typeset, to be dropped into the page at the last moment.

I used to wonder why the chaps who wrote down the scores were always from Accounts. I suppose it was because it involved numbers - usually a 1 or a 2, sometimes a 3 or, in Sheffield Wednesday's case, mostly a 0. A couple of years into my career as a copy boy, with Ray indisposed, I was given the weighty responsibility (for one afternoon only) of reading out the scores. Obviously, this "Boy!" was going places.

As I started the sixth form, with the idea of becoming a journalist still bouncing around in my head, my dad spotted an advertisement that had been placed in *The Star* by the *South Yorkshire Times*. They wanted a junior reporter, and I decided to apply.

At the start of the Seventies, it wasn't unknown for regional journalists to begin their careers at 16, straight after O-levels, although the industry was moving towards a minimum qualification of two A-levels. In the regional press, graduates were still a relatively rare breed. I was invited for interview and, wearing my only suit and my dad's overcoat, I set off for Mexborough, a mining town near Doncaster, for the first and probably the last time in my life.

The interview was conducted in the early evening, when all the staff except the editor, Dick Ridyard, had left for the day. Before being appointed editor two years previously, Ridyard had been the paper's chief reporter and sports editor. Like many regional editors, he was a mainstay of the local community and had a lifelong commitment to training, later serving on the National Council for the Training of Journalists.

On a gloomy night, in his gloomy office next door to Mexborough's gloomy railway station, he put me at my ease with a few softball questions and then...gave me a spelling test. I got them all right except 'possess', as Ridyard pointed out to me. A case of interview nerves, obviously. Despite my mistake, he wrote a few days later to offer me the job. After a long chat with my parents, we agreed the best course was to stay at school and finish my A-levels, so I turned down the offer. It was undoubtedly the right decision – as a wet-behind-the-ears 16-year-old, I wasn't ready for the world of work.

Around a year later, journalism reared its head again as a career choice, and this time it was for keeps. Now in the upper sixth, I replied to an advertisement for the One-Year Pre-Entry Course in Journalism, run by Richmond College, Sheffield. After a day of tests and group discussions, I was interviewed by the college's sub-editing guru Frank Littlewood and *Morning Telegraph* editorial executive Ken Morgan. Things seemed to me to be going well until Morgan's final question: 'Have you ever thought of becoming a policeman?' I was thrown, and stuttered: "Er, no, I haven't. Why do you ask?"

"Well, you have a steady demeanour. You look as though you'd fit in well with the police." I went away convinced this was his way of gently preparing me for a rejection letter but a few days later I received the offer of a place. I was in, much to the disgust of my French teacher, Mrs Godber, who revealed she had me earmarked for university, followed by a job as a translator at the European parliament. I can honestly say I never look back on that conversation and think: "If only ..."

As if the joy of winning a place wasn't enough, *The Star* then advertised that it was looking to sponsor a number of trainees on the course. Editor Colin Brannigan, newly-appointed chairman of the NCTJ's training committee, put quite a lot of the company's money where his mouth was by offering five sponsored places. After another set of tests and an interview with *The Star*'s assistant editor Peter Goodman, I was offered a traineeship.

This couldn't get any better. Only it did, when the city council gave me a one-off £50 grant. Bankrolled by *The Star*, with work experience built in during college holidays and a job guaranteed at the end of it, no tuition fees, and even a few quid from the local authority. Added to that, I would be living rent-free with my parents, so – apart from beer and the odd post-pub pie and chips – I had no subsistence costs either. And I had a part-time bar job, which meant I could afford to run a car. (If you were expecting a bleak tale of student poverty, look away now).

The name of the pub where I worked was the Norfolk Arms but it was known universally as Dodger's, after a previous landlord. He was given his nickname on account of his prodigious nose. By way of explanation, a helpful regular told me: "It were that big, when 'e turned 'is 'ead, yer'd 'ave ter duck ter dodge it". Years later, the brewery renamed the pub Dodger's, and erected a new sign, depicting the former landlord and his humungous hooter.

The pub was across the road from Sheffield's main bus garage and just a couple of minutes' walk from the city's Midland railway station, so was a regular watering hole for drivers and conductors who had just finished their shift. On Thursday – pay day – the tap room in Dodger's would resound to the noise of Caribbean busmen slamming down a winning domino, with an almighty flourish. The pub's licence allowed small-stakes gaming, but the stakes in these games were often far from small. It wasn't unknown for a week's wages to be blown in an hour or two.

I'd heard about the bar job from my Uncle Jack, a Dodger's regular. At the weekend, Jack and his pals - a mix of labourers and lorry drivers - would don tailor-made suits, collar and tie, their shoes polished to a parade-ground shine (a legacy of their years of National Service) and hit the town. They would always finish the night at Dodger's, where a lock-in was a nailed-on certainty.

The downside of my pub job was that I worked every Friday, Saturday and Sunday evening, plus Sunday lunchtime. What I missed at weekends I would attempt to make up for on Tuesday nights with my college mates at the nearby Samantha's nite spot. Although, to be honest, Samantha's on a Tuesday could make City Road cemetery seem lively.

* * * *

Driving an ancient, red Mini and sporting burgundy-coloured wet-look shoes and a pair of grey loon pants,* I looked every inch the cool student on my first day at Richmond College of Further Education.

Perched on a hill overlooking the Richmond housing estate, the college was one of seven around the country that ran journalism courses accredited by the National Council for the Training of Journalists. The building was low-slung and Sixties built – eerily similar to the school, just a mile away, which I'd left three months earlier.

Richmond boasts some well-known former students, including investigative journalist John Sweeney, BBC golf correspondent Iain Carter and TV motormouth Jeremy Clarkson, who was sent on an eight-week block-release course by his first paper, the *Rotherham Advertiser*, to learn the rudiments of journalism. In addition to these luminaries, over the course of more than 20 years Richmond was the launchpad for hundreds of other fledgling journalists.

The Class of '74 have plied their trade far and wide; on regional and national newspapers in the UK, Australia, Bermuda, Hong Kong and the Far East; on TV and radio; as magazine journalists; as sports reporters; as travel writers; and as senior executives. Richmond gave us a great grounding.

*Spray-on tight to the knee, exploding into 28-inch bell bottoms, loon pants were the flariest of flared trousers. Often paired (though never in my case) with a garishly-coloured tank top.

My year at the college began in the autumn of 1973, as prog rock met glam rock and the mullet ruled the hairwaves. We would-be newshounds found ourselves rubbing shoulders with students on a wide range of vocational courses. Richmond was particularly strong on secretarial studies, which meant there were shorthand teachers on tap, whose mission was to get the journalism students to 100 words per minute by the end of the course. For most secretarial students, 100 wpm was a stroll in the park but for many on the journalism course it was like being asked to scale Everest. And six weeks into our course, the mountain confronting us became decidedly steeper.

Editor of *The Star*, Colin Brannigan, was outraged to learn that his trainees were being taught Teeline, a newer, easier-to-learn form of shorthand, which subsequently has become the de facto standard for journalists. Brannigan was having none of this nonsense and insisted his five sponsored students must be taught the classic Pitman system. Teaching two different versions of shorthand in parallel was a timetabling impossibility for the college, so Brannigan's demand meant, in effect, all 25 students on the journalism course would have to abandon Teeline and start all over again with Pitman.

To add insult to injury, the college staff decided the only way we could possibly master a harder system and have any hope of reaching 100 wpm in the time available was to introduce an extra shorthand session, from 6pm to 9pm every Monday night. When this news broke, the popularity of the *Star*'s five sponsored trainees – already seen as the Little Lord Fauntleroys of the course – took something of a dip.

In addition to attending lectures, we journalism students were expected to find stories around college, for publication in the *Richmond Reporter* – a weekly, A5-sized newspaper which editor and senior lecturer Gerry Kreibich claimed proudly was the world's smallest newspaper.

The *Reporter* was a labour of love for Gerry. Every Tuesday, he would take home one of the college's enormous golf-ball typewriters and would get up at 4am to type out the last of that week's stories and write the headlines, in order that the edition was ready to be printed by the college's technical staff first thing on Wednesday morning. We didn't know it at the time but as my friends and I were spilling out of Samantha's nite spot, Gerry was beavering away, to ensure our earliest, faltering attempts at journalism would reach an audience.

My first-ever front-page splash was in the *Reporter* (dateline: October 31, 1973). It revealed that the nearby Springwood pub was doing a booming trade in lunches because students were unimpressed with the college's catering. (It had nothing to do with the pub's wide selection of draught ales and lagers, obviously). I interviewed landlord 'Slim' Shiel at the bar and, with no notebook to hand, scribbled my notes on the back of a fag packet. It was a pack of ten Player's No.6, belonging to my fellow student and friend Will Venters.

Will went on to have a successful and varied career in print journalism, radio, PR and TV, mostly in the West Yorkshire region. He died in 2012, aged just 56. A few years later his name cropped up in unexpected circumstances. My wife Jo and I were at the John Smith's Stadium for the 2017 Championship play-off semi-final between Huddersfield Town and Sheffield Wednesday. Our son Rory – then a football reporter at the Huddersfield Examiner – had picked up a couple of spare tickets for us.

Before the match kicked off, we began chatting to the man sitting next to us. He was a local, of a similar age to me, who told us he lived in London but retained a season ticket and came back to West Yorkshire for all of Huddersfield's home games. There was an empty seat next to him, which he explained was his mother's. She had died a couple of weeks earlier.

As we chatted, it emerged that he had been Will's best friend at school. We exchanged tales about Will, had a few laughs and both of us became quite emotional. As the game kicked off, he said: "Well, this is fate. Town are bound to win now." The match was drawn, as was the return leg at Hillsborough, but Town won after a penalty shoot-out, which took them to Wembley for the play-off final. After another nail-biting shoot-out, little Huddersfield Town were promoted to the Premier League. Even their manager said it was a miracle. How Will would have loved it.

As well as teaching us the basics of the journalist's craft – newspaper law, local government, journalism practice and the inescapable shorthand – the Richmond lecturers were keen to prepare us for newsroom life by giving us a taste of the real world and getting us to write about it. Visits to magistrates' court, local council meetings, police and fire stations were all on the agenda, as one might expect of a journalism course. There was also a memorable and fortuitously-timed day trip to the Houses of Parliament, when we squeezed into the Strangers' Gallery to hear Prime Minister Edward Heath announce that he was calling a General Election. But the trip that left the greatest impression on me was a visit to a coal mine. On his blog dedicated to the

Richmond journalism course, Gerry Kreibich describes one of the many colliery visits he led:

"Once, having delivered the spiel about the forthcoming experience, complete with blackboard diagrams of cages in mine-shafts and miles of subterranean tunnels, I dismissed a class of pre-entry students and set off for lunch. Realising that I had forgotten my briefcase, I returned to the apparently-empty classroom and was startled to hear a scraping sound and see one of the tables moving slightly. Stooping, I spotted a red-faced student on all fours making his laborious way between the steel table-legs. He emerged, flustered. 'I was just seeing what it would be like at the coal-face,' he explained. It was pretty good preparation, as it turned out – two days later the students found themselves crouched in that very pose, hundreds of feet beneath the ground. But this was no quiet classroom. It was, as one student later described it, like a scene from hell.

"A spike-toothed cutting wheel screamed and clattered past, only a few feet away; shiny dust sparkled in the air; jagged black slabs as big as TV sets fell from the roof along the newly-ripped line of the coal-face; a dozen students cowered between the steel pit-props that supported the shiny black ceiling a few inches above them; and the miners – visible only as white eyes and red lips – bellowed unintelligible messages over the unspeakable uproar.

"As the cutter fell silent, the newly-gained coal rumbled away on a conveyor belt towards the distant exit shaft. And the students met a solitary figure whose job it was to step forward into virgin territory and plant the explosive charges that would begin the next assault on this layer of black gold beneath South Yorkshire. They looked with awe at this bluff, black-faced fellow with explosives at his command. 'Unbelievable,' muttered one lad.

"Back on the surface there were hot showers and refreshments. (In the obvious absence of women's showers, the girls were privileged to use the ablutions reserved for managers and deputies). Cans of beer, plates of sandwiches and a giant pot of tea awaited at what we were pleased to call a press conference – a chance for the students to fire questions at a senior colliery official. It was normally someone who had been underground with us, unrecognisable now in suit and collar and tie. Questions flowed freely and the students took notes from which to write 350 words back in the classroom."

A few weeks after our colliery excursion, we visited a Sheffield steel mill, which left a similarly deep impression. From our vantage point high on a gantry, we peered down on an oppressively dark, monochrome, Tolkienesque world, where workers scurried purposefully about their business, dwarfed by gigantic vats of molten metal and white-hot, spark-spitting girders. For the steelmen, it was just another day at work. For us, it was another of those scenes from hell, but this time we were 40 feet above the ground rather than 1,500 feet beneath it. I felt extremely grateful to be heading towards a career of well-lit, centrally-heated comfort.

As we neared the end of our course, Kreibich asked the group what ambitions we had as journalists. Humility prevented many from sharing their thoughts. But it didn't stop me. I declared that I wanted to work on a national newspaper, to prove I could hack it at the highest level, and, eventually, to edit a regional evening. Was it just me or did someone mutter the word 'smartarse'?

Chapter Four

Spies, Highs and Meat Pies

Some journalists enter the trade because it's their calling. They are on a mission to inform; determined to speak truth to power; to stand up for what's right; to comfort the afflicted and afflict the comfortable. In my case, it was because I was pretty good at English and there was a chance it might make me a bit more interesting to the opposite sex.

One of the advertising reps at *The Star* had latched on to the same idea, and would deploy "Hi, I'm a reporter" as his standard chat-up line. I guess he'd realised that "Hi, would you like to buy an advert?" didn't have quite the same ring to it.

The irony here was that, as a new-boy reporter, I had the sexier job but was to be seen tootling up to assignments in a green Morris Traveller* with nearly 200,000 miles on the clock. I'd bought it from the company for £200 when they pensioned it off, its years of service as a newspaper delivery workhorse done. In the winter months, I would emerge from my dependably dull vehicle wearing a blue duffle coat and a yards-long red-and-blue scarf that wouldn't have looked out of place on Tom Baker as Dr Who. The outfit did the job but was unlikely to get me on the front cover of *Tailor & Cutter* magazine.

Meanwhile my advertising colleague could be seen sporting a sleek sheepskin overcoat and driving a purple Lotus Europa – a 1.6-litre, mid-engined virility statement, guaranteed to turn the head of every eligible young lady in the South Yorkshire travel-to-work district.

The ad man and I got on well enough and we both played for Telstar, the *Sheffield Telegraph & Star*'s not-very-good football team. After a while, I noticed that at our Sunday morning games his car would almost always be parked next to mine. I suspect it wasn't a coincidence.

* *Aka a shooting break. A small estate car with wood panels down the sides and back. It wasn't cool then but, strangely, it is now.*

Fresh from our college course, the five sponsored trainees (plus one graduate recruit, for good luck) were tipped into *The Star*'s newsroom. And there we sat. With a complement of 20-odd senior news reporters, there wasn't enough work to keep the six new starters fully occupied*. I spent much of my time writing one and two-paragraph fillers or shadowing senior colleagues as they went about their reporting business. In my case at least, the cuttings book our college lecturers had recommended we should keep was seeing precious little action.

One of my rare forays out of the office in these early months was to attend my first inquest, which was into the death of a baby. The hearing was held in a small room, perhaps ten or 12 feet square, at the coroner's court building. There were six people present – the coroner, the coroner's officer, the baby's parents, a senior reporter from *The Star* and me, as his shadow.

The coroner handled the proceedings with great compassion as the bereaved parents sobbed quietly, the baby's father draping a consoling arm around his wife's shoulder. Sitting just a few feet away from them, I felt like an intruder. Meanwhile, my colleague's main interest was his shaving cut, which he dabbed constantly, every now and then inspecting his blood-spotted Kleenex.

Journalists have to learn to detach themselves from emotional situations, otherwise we would be incapable of doing our job, but I wondered if his performance was perhaps for effect, to show me what a battle-hardened hack he was. The press has a right to attend courts, including coroners' courts – it's a fundamental principle of open justice, and I support it entirely. But, increasingly, I ask myself how much value there is in covering stories of sad, intimate loss such as the one I witnessed on my first experience of a coroner's inquest. I also ask myself if, in that tiny room, I was being overly sensitive. Or was my colleague just being a heartless prat?

*Most journalists working today would shake their head in disbelief at the idea of a newsroom where there's not enough work to do.

One of the best pieces of advice for young reporters is to develop the skill of 'thinking like a reader'. I learned that lesson in slightly embarrassing circumstances when covering a story about a Sheffield café whose home-made meat and potato pie had been judged the Best in Yorkshire. News editor David Mastin briefed me to drive to the café, in the working-class district of Wadsley, eat a portion of the highly-praised pie and interview the women who had won the award. As reporting assignments go, I've known worse.

The two middle-aged piemakers, both in floral pinafores, were lovely. They were surprised their humble business, based in a row of small, local shops, had been singled out for such an accolade. They were delighted that their local paper was interested and they gave me some nice quotes. And the pie, served with mushy peas and a splash of the classic Sheffield accompaniment, Henderson's Relish*, was lovely, too. Back at the office, with a full belly and feeling very content, I filed my story, which included a rapturous description of the crisp shortcrust pastry, the succulent beef, the tender potatoes and the silky gravy. All in all, I was pretty pleased with myself.

A few minutes later, Mastin called me over. "This pie story. Did you ask them for the recipe?" Er, no, David. "Don't you think our readers might want to know how to make the best pie in the county?" Er, yes David. "So get me the recipe." The café didn't have a phone, which meant a tail-between-the-legs return trip to Wadsley. From then on, whatever story I was covering, I would ask myself: "What's the 'pie recipe question' here?", to make sure I didn't miss the crucial piece of information our readers would want to know.

Ten years later, at the *Telegraph & Argus*, in Bradford, we were running a cooking competition in conjunction with a local Asian restaurant. Time to wheel out the "what's the recipe?" question again – this time in relation to the chef's chicken tikka masala. The chef obliged, we ran the recipe in the Saturday edition and the readers loved it. That simple ten-paragraph piece generated the biggest reader response of any article I've published (apart from the time I screwed up the answers to our bumper Christmas crossword).

Made in Sheffield since 1885 to a secret recipe, 'Hendo's' is also excellent on chips or cheese on toast. It's a bit like Worcester sauce, only much, much better.

It was one of those rare occasions as a journalist when big news happens right on your doorstep. At around 6.30am, my mum was making breakfast when she shouted to me that there was something odd going on across the road. I looked out of the kitchen window to see several police cars and small groups of neighbours, some still in their night clothes, standing in the street. I phoned the newsdesk, who told me they were aware there had been an incident but didn't have any details yet.

By the time I got to the office at 7.30, the story had broken. In the middle of the night, a young woman had slipped downstairs to the garden shed and removed a vice from the workbench. She took it indoors and wrapped it in a towel. Then she crept into her sleeping father's bedroom and battered his brains out.

In the months leading up to the fateful night, I would often see her walking the short distance from the bus stop to home. We had known each other as children but these days she never spoke. Her blonde hair was lank, she was thin and looked unkempt. Even in the height of summer, she wore a beige, faux-leather coat, buttoned up to the neck and belted.

As the court case later revealed, she, her sisters and her mother had lived a nightmare life with a violent man. The neighbours talked of furious rows and several said they had witnessed the girl's father holding down his wife on a patch of grass near their house, with a knife to her throat. After their mother died, her elder sisters moved out one by one until she was left her alone with her abusive father.

When the case came to court it was covered by *The Star*'s Crown Court reporter Peter Evans, a gifted writer with the ability to distil a mass of detailed evidence into a few hundred words of compelling prose. On the day of the trial, the intro to his front-page splash began: "A golden-haired girl of 22 ...."

I decided not to tell the newsdesk that ten years or so earlier the golden-haired girl had been a regular visitor to our house. She would accompany her older sister, a school friend of my cousin, who was our Saturday night babysitter. She always seemed happy and talkative – very different from the haunted young woman she would become. I knew that if I revealed this titbit, I would be asked to write a first-person piece, along the lines of: "My babysitter became a killer". For the sake of a few quickly-forgotten paragraphs, I wasn't prepared to do that. It would have felt like a betrayal.

A few months later, there was a macabre coda to the story. At the time, Gleadless Valley was still a desirable place to live, and the city council had a long list of people wanting to move there. But the story of the 'murder house', as it became known locally, put off many potential tenants, and it remained unoccupied. Eventually, a friend of a friend moved in with his young family. He had been well down the waiting list so when the house was offered to him, he jumped at it. The murder didn't bother him, he told me, but he would need to buy some paint - the coat of emulsion the council decorators had applied to the bedroom wall hadn't quite masked the bloodstains.

* * * *

I'd been a trainee reporter for six months or so when I was asked to take part in a survey by the National Union of Journalists, who wanted to take the temperature of newcomers to the industry. It asked what job you would have done, had you not become a journalist (Answer: PE teacher), and whether you thought you'd be happier doing that rather than being a journalist (Answer: Yes). When I wrote that, it brought me up short. I wasn't unhappy at work but I wasn't terribly happy either. That season's glut of trainees meant I wasn't getting many good stories and very little of my work was getting into the paper. Put bluntly, I was bored.

So it came as a relief when I was sent to *The Star*'s Chesterfield office 'for a minimum of six months', as stipulated in my training contract. The 'minimum six months' turned into a year and a half spent learning on the job and having a lot of fun. Under the guidance of chief reporter Glyn Williams, my confidence began to grow.

Glyn's claim to reporting fame was that his story lifted the lid on the notorious Rhino Whip Affair. It was 1963, and Glyn was the only reporter in court when an apparently mundane remand hearing before Sheffield magistrates took a sensational turn. After the prosecution had made their case to have a man accused of burglary held in custody, the defence solicitor asked his client to take off his shirt. He did so, to reveal a pattern of livid welts and bruises across his back. When his solicitor asked him who had inflicted the injuries, he pointed to one of the policemen in court. The accused man and two other burglary suspects claimed they had been beaten with a rhino whip, to extract their confessions.

The case exposed a corrupt culture that stemmed from the highest levels of Sheffield City Police. Detectives were encouraged by senior officers to beat suspects and to doctor evidence to gain convictions. After Glyn's report was published, the case was picked up by *The Star*'s sister paper, the *Morning Telegraph*, which led a celebrated editorial campaign to reveal the full extent of the misconduct. After a public tribunal, four senior officers were suspended, including Chief Constable Eric Staines and Head of CID George Carnill, both of whom retired within days.

Twelve years later, Glyn was plying his trade in the calmer waters of Chesterfield, a market town 12 miles from Sheffield, just over the county border in Derbyshire. He led a team of five, based in an office above a newsagent's shop and overlooking the market square. Glyn was one of the most solid, even-handed reporters I've known, so it was a shock when he was summoned to the offices of North East Derbyshire District Council, to be confronted by senior councillors who were angry about his coverage.

He set off for the meeting looking concerned, but when he returned the dark clouds had dispersed. The leader of the council had opened the meeting by accusing him of not reporting what she said. Glyn responded that this was a serious allegation against a journalist and asked her to cite examples. The complaint dissolved when she said: "Well, it's not that you don't report what I say, but you don't report what I mean."

With our own edition to fill every day, there was more than enough work to keep four reporters and photographer Brian Vaughan busy. In summer, with holidays and days off, I might be on my own in the office, having to decide what to cover, how much time to spend on each story and making sure there was enough content to fill our pages. By the time I returned to head office, I had passed my senior reporter's exams, felt confident in my ability and was looking forward to the future. The school playing fields would have to wait.

While my spell in Chesterfield was the making of me as a reporter, life in a branch office doesn't suit everyone. *The Star*'s chief reporter Ron Roland enjoyed telling the tale of a new recruit by the name of Petts, a Southerner who was lured north for the first time in his life, to take a reporting job in *The Star*'s Barnsley office. Apparently, Mr Petts was something of an aesthete, which would have marked him out as unusual in a tough mining town not renowned for its cultural hinterland.

On his first day in Barnsley, Petts didn't file anything. The newsdesk assumed he was taking a little time to find his feet. Day 2 came and went – still no copy, and they couldn't raise him on phone, either. When the silence persisted into Day 3, Roland sent a head office reporter to Barnsley, to find out what was going on. The office was empty but in a typewriter was a hand-written message which read: "Returned South. Regrets. Petts."

Comings and goings have always been part of newsroom life, as ambitious staff seek to make their way up the editorial food chain. But when I returned to head office from Chesterfield, one particularly short-lived career was the talk of the reporting pool.

A few months earlier, a young man with no previous connection to journalism had been given a job as a reporter. It turned out he was the son of a diplomat, whose next-door neighbour just happened to be the top dog in United Newspapers, our parent company. The newcomer struggled, both journalistically and socially, and after a few months he made a sudden, unexplained exit. Rumours swirled regarding the reason for his departure but, despite heavy pressure to spill the gossip, the news editors remained steadfastly tight-lipped.

A few weeks later, *Private Eye* revealed that the missing reporter had been escorted to an airport by an editorial executive and shepherded on to a plane, to be met by his father on landing. The *Eye* suggested, intriguingly, that during his time at *The Star* the young man had developed a taste for "quaffing draught cough medicine". The desk he had vacated remained unoccupied until reporter Ian Lyness joined *The Star* a few months later. On his first morning, Lyness unlocked the desk to find it crammed with half-consumed bottles of Gees Linctus, an over-the-counter cough remedy containing tincture of opium. As an office wag put it: "That lad wasn't much good as a reporter but I never heard him cough once."

After his bizarre first-day experience, Lyness settled into the team quickly. An urbane north Londoner with a strong interest in showbusiness, he would occasionally drop into conversation that, at 6ft 4in, he was 'the same height as Clint Eastwood', one of his Hollywood heroes.

Ian went on to cover showbiz for the United Newspapers group – for whom he interviewed Eastwood – and later for the *Daily Express*. He told me an amusing story from his time on a weekly paper, where he worked for an "aggressive creep" of a news editor who took pleasure in making his staff's life as difficult as possible. One of Ian's colleagues took his revenge elegantly by submitting a regular expense claim for "Entertaining Mr Sloane", confident that his boorish boss would never have heard of the Joe Orton play and would assume 'Mr Sloane' was one of the reporter's local contacts.

* * * *

As a regional reporter, one of the things that's guaranteed to make your heart sink is being asked to follow up a story from your patch that's been broken by a national paper. More often than not, it results in a wild goose chase. And so it proved when the news editor sent me to the village of Over Haddon, in the hills overlooking Bakewell, Derbyshire, to check out a short story tucked away in the *Daily Express*'s William Hickey gossip column. It claimed Sir Maurice Oldfield – then the director of MI6 and the inspiration for 'M' in James Bond – had got engaged to a West End showgirl.

From the off, it didn't smell right. True, "the spymaster and the showgirl" was a great story – so why only one paragraph, buried in the gossip column? Then there was the 40-year age gap, and the fact that Oldfield was a "confirmed bachelor", as the euphemism goes. But, following the newsdesk's instructions, I fired up my VW Beetle and headed for Over Haddon, where Derbyshire-born Sir Maurice owned a house.

The Star cuttings file contained a story describing a "vow of silence" the villagers had pledged to uphold, should any strangers turn up asking questions about their neighbour. Sure enough, after I'd knocked on a few doors, the net curtains started to twitch. Nobody slammed a door in my face but it was abundantly clear there was no hope anyone would talk. Finally, I found someone – the owner of the local grocery store – who was happy to chat, but he had only recently moved to the village and there was nothing worthwhile he could tell me. For Over Haddon, it was over and out.

Next stop was the NatWest bank, in Bakewell, where I'd been told Oldfield's younger brother worked. He came outside to speak to me but only to let me know, politely but firmly, that he had nothing to say about the *Express story* or his brother.

I decided to head back to the office, but when I got to the public car park I found my VW blocked in by a police car. Two burly (actually, enormous), plain-clothes officers got out and asked who I was and why I'd been asking questions. I showed them my Press card, told them I was following up a story and they could check my credentials with my news editor. They accepted what I'd told them and one of them said: "OK Neil, you'll be going back to

Sheffield now." I said I might have a few more enquiries to make but he told me, for the avoidance of any doubt: "No. You ARE going back to Sheffield." For the first four miles of the journey back to the city, they very kindly provided me with a police escort.

* * * *

Sometimes, exclusive stories are the culmination of months of hard slog, and sometimes they fall into your lap. I happened to be in the right place at the right time when the newsdesk needed someone to chase a tip-off that two girls had been suspended from school for poisoning their headmaster's tea.

The tip had come from an impeccable source – a Church of England rector who had experience as a freelance reporter. He also happened to be our deputy chief sub's brother. The rector was on the board of governors at the school, in the North Derbyshire village of Clowne, where the 14-year-old girls had spiked the head's afternoon cuppa with an assortment of chemicals they had taken from the chemistry lab. The head needed a couple of days off school but had made a full recovery, while the two pupils had been suspended.

I drove to the village to meet the rector, who gave me chapter and verse. The only proviso: the story must not be traceable to him as the source. So I needed to find someone who would stand up the story and give me an on-the-record quote, but I soon discovered the governors and school staff had been sworn to silence. I chatted to parents at the school gates but either they didn't know anything or weren't prepared to spill the beans.

As a final shot, I found the address of the chair of governors and called round to see her, on the slim chance that she might confirm the story. There was no reply, and a neighbour informed me she was on a week's holiday and wasn't expected back until late that night.

As I searched for a phone box to let the newsdesk know I'd drawn a blank, it dawned on me that as she'd been away for a week, the chair of governors would not have been at the meeting where it was decided to stonewall the press. But now they were aware a reporter was sniffing around, there was a risk that one of her colleagues would speak to her before I did. So, bright and early the next morning, I knocked on the door of her caravan home. She answered, still in her dressing gown and curlers. I told her I was a reporter from *The Star* and asked if she could confirm the story. "Oh yes, love. Come in and have a cup of tea ..."

Chapter Five

The Grey Cardigans

If reporters are the Cavaliers of journalism, fearlessly seeking out news with a devil-may-care *élan*, the sub-editors are the humourless Roundheads, who take a sneering delight in butchering the reporters' gilded prose.

Subs inhabit a monochrome world, where frugality is a quality to be celebrated (but only in strict moderation) and small pleasures are derived from tut-tutting about misused grammar and repairing infinitives that have been carelessly split. From the very first day, the subs' desk felt like my natural home.

My switch to the production side of journalism was not so much a career move as a bolt out of the blue. It was prompted by a staffing crisis on the subs' desk, which editor Colin Brannigan solved by shipping three of his senior reporters across the office. This was the quickest way to provide urgently-needed subbing firepower, while filling three reporting roles would be no problem all. The slight issue, though, was that the likely lads who moved across the office had a total of two weeks' subbing experience between us.

The large, horseshoe-shaped subs' desk dominated the centre of the *Sheffield Telegraph* and *Star* newsroom. By day it was occupied by the *Star* subbing team, who would vacate it around 4.30pm when their *Morning Telegraph* colleagues arrived for their shift. Deputy chief sub Malcolm Harris sat at the centre, on the inside of the horseshoe curve, with a herd of perhaps a dozen subs scattered around him. Viking-bearded Malcolm was a man of few words; if he thought you were taking too long to sub a story, he would simply hurl the next one in your direction. Followed by another one.

To Malcolm's far left were the elder statesmen, who were mostly called Ron. There was Ron Hankinson, who was known as Hank, and Ron Wilkinson, who was known as ... Ron. Looking back, it seems amazing that a bunch of professional headline writers didn't christen them The Two Ronnies.

Hank smoked cigarettes and sported a grey, V-neck sweater; Ron favoured a pipe and a grey cardigan – the classic sub-editing attire in newsrooms all over the UK. A man of great experience and patience, Ron had taught me the rudiments of subbing as part of my junior journalist training. His daughter Debbie Coxon – another of *The Star*'s five sponsored trainees – recalled that, for many years, the two Rons played continuous games of paper chess. "One would write his move on a piece of copy paper, push it across the desk, and next day the other would return the move,'"Debbie told me. "Dad used to say they'd played 300-odd games and he'd won 299!"

Many years later, Debbie told me that she had volunteered to transfer to the subs' desk but the idea was rejected because, as a newsroom executive explained: "Some of the older reporters wouldn't like their copy subbed by a woman."

The trio at the Rons' end of the desk was completed by Clive Frith, a man who didn't believe in letting things go to waste. My mum would have described him as "careful". Every day, after the reporters had clocked off, Clive would make a sweep of their desks and pour any unused sugar from the day's teas and coffees into a 2lb Tate & Lyle bag, which he kept in his desk. When full, it would be taken home. This daily ritual was a source of constant amusement for the news editors and reinforced their already dim view of the sub-editing classes. But that didn't seem to bother Clive. Careful is as careful does.

The other end of the subs' desk had a more Bohemian flavour, its two fixtures being former chief sub Ollie Fox, who could switch from genial to acidic and back again in the blink of an eye, and Charlie Bingham – sub-editor by day, jazz drummer by night. Ollie was a pipe man while Charlie would oscillate between his pipe and a packet of fags, depending on how the mood took him. These two seemed like good fun, and I opted to sit at their end.

The subs' lunch break was just 45 minutes, starting at 11.30am, in order that everyone would be back in their seat to work on the change pages for the main City edition. On the stroke of half past eleven, Ollie, Charlie and Malcolm would decamp, either to their "summer quarters" (the Brown Bear) or 'winter quarters' (the slightly nearer Three Cranes) for a lunch of three swift pints apiece. Food didn't enter the equation.

With a five-minute walk each way, that meant a maximum of 35 minutes' drinking time. After a month or two on the desk, I would join them a couple of times a week. For me, the City edition came and went in a blur. In hindsight, this seems highly unprofessional, but - in my defence - these were the days when it wasn't unknown for regional newspapers to have a staff bar on the premises. (I'm looking at you, *Coventry Evening Telegraph*).

The popular characterisation of subs as the grey men of journalism is, of course, grossly unfair. Many have interesting back-stories – none more so than Tom Dobney, the unassuming and unfailingly-helpful deputy art editor at the *Daily Express*, who, at the age of 15, gained the distinction of becoming the world's youngest military pilot.

Soon after the Battle of Britain, as a result of a dare by a schoolmate, Tom falsified his birth certificate and – aided and abetted by his divorced mother – joined the Royal Air Force Military Reserve. He made his first solo flight just six days after his fifteenth birthday and soon earned his wings. A matter of months later, he found himself in command of a bomber crew, based in Oxfordshire. By chance, his father found out and alerted the RAF, who discharged him immediately.

But young Tom was no quitter. Later that year he re-enlisted, again claiming to be 18. Again, he was found out. Eventually, he joined up lawfully and by 1948, at the ripe old age of 21, he was flying transport aircraft in the Berlin airlift. He went on to work in the Metropolitan Police and as an RAF runway controller before landing on the *Express* art desk. Not quite your standard career flightpath.

If Tom was one of the quiet men of the *Express*, long-serving night editor Claude Lescure was a legend in his own lifetime. He had gone off to war as a naïve youngster and returned as a battle-hardened reporter, having served in the Army press corps across Europe. He went on to clock up 50 years in the news business and was a consummate production journalist.

Claude was partial to a gin. Not just any old gin – it had to be Cork Distillery Company gin. After his shift at the *Express*, he would decamp to the Manchester Press Club, where he would sit in the same seat at the corner of the bar – named Claude's Corner, in his honour – and hold court while consuming several large CDCs and tonic. As a surprise gift to mark Claude's 50 years as a journalist, editor Tony Fowler arranged for him to visit to the CDC distillery, where he was treated in a manner befitting his status as their Most Valuable Customer.

Claude, who lost an eye in a childhood accident, always wore the same black suit, shiny with age, which earned him the nickname among composing room staff of The One-Eyed Crow. Despite the nickname, the notoriously hard-to-impress compositors held him in the highest regard.

Legend has it that when he had been fitted with a new glass eye, Claude was so pleased with the result he wanted to tell the world about it. In the composing room, he explained that the eye was constructed from a special type of glass, which made it indestructible. One compositor wasn't convinced and wanted to put it to the test. So Claude popped out the eye and placed it on the stone (the metal work surface where pages were put together). The Doubting Thomas picked up a mallet and brought it down with all the force he could muster, causing the "indestructible" eye to shatter into a thousand tiny fragments. The One-Eyed Crow wasn't crowing now.

The *Express* sports department had its share of characters, too. Bryn Davies, black-haired and jam-jar-spectacled, had a deserved reputation as the best headline writer on the desk. He was also partial to a drink, which could lead to fun and games when he returned from his mid-shift break.

One afternoon, I arrived in the office to see Bryn locked in a furious argument across the newsroom with a reporter who was intent on winding him up. The whole staff was spellbound as Bryn stood at his desk and launched into a stream of slurred invective, to which the reporter who had been baiting him had no answer. Unfortunately, as he was about to apply his verbal *coup de grâce*, Bryn's trousers fell down. More unfortunately still, he wasn't wearing underpants.

Among the strong Scottish contingent, Friday nights at the *Express* had something of a party atmosphere. In the Seventies, the company had decided to close its production centre in Glasgow, as a cost-saving measure. Those news and sports subs who weren't ready to take redundancy relocated to Manchester, from where the Scottish edition was now produced.

Every Friday night, the news editor of the *Scottish Sunday Express*, who was still based in Glasgow, travelled to Manchester to help with production of the weekend's edition. He would arrive in the newsroom carrying plastic bags bulging with coronary-inducing delicacies such as square sausage, white pudding and Scotch pies, which he would distribute to his grateful countrymen. For the displaced Sons of Caledonia, this little ritual was the undisputed highlight of the week.

Some of the skills that were essential elements of the sub's armoury in those old-tech days were made obsolete by computerisation. One of the core techniques was "casting off" – accurately estimating the length of the story you were subbing, taking into account the typeface, type sizes and column width, so that it fitted the space allocated in the page.

The best subs took great pride in their casting off, and would get it right with amazing consistency. For others, casting off was a permanently-closed book but at least it kept the stone subs* in work. For page designers, a slide rule was an essential piece of kit for sizing and cropping pictures. While computerisation took away much of the drudge of subbing, and arguably gave the sub more time to concentrate on the story itself, a part of me pines for these lost arts.

Another sub-editing skill that has been all but lost is the contents bill – those A-framed billboards we used see outside every newsagent's shop, promoting the best stories in that day's paper. The general rule regarding contents bills was that they should be no longer than five words, and the words should be short, so they could be blown up to maximum size when printed, to catch the passing reader's eye. For regional titles, this was one of the most effective ways of marketing their content, whether it be news, sport or the big classified advertising categories. "1,000 jobs in tonight's *Chronicle*" sent a powerful "buy me" message to readers.

The key to an effective bill is to tell just enough of the story to whet the reader's appetite without giving the whole game away, and so entice them to buy a copy. My assistant editor at the *Newcastle Chronicle*, Roger Borrell, gave a perfect example of how to turn a bad news bill into a good one. A young child had been missing for several days and the whole of Tyneside was on tenterhooks, wondering if she was alive or dead. Just before the Saturday edition went to press, she was found. The bill written by one of our subs read:

BABY ALICE FOUND ALIVE

*Sub-editors based in the composing room who were the last line of editorial defence. Their role was to correct the cock-ups missed (and sometimes made) by their colleagues earlier in the subbing process.

Roger had the nous to remove the final word, which made all the difference. The version that appeared on the streets – and drove significant extra sales – read:

BABY ALICE FOUND

When the day's news bills had been written by the subs, they were sent to the newspaper sales department, where the wording would be either typed or hand-written on an A1-sized sheet. Unfortunately, the more steps there are in a process, the greater the chance something can go wrong. On one never-to-be-forgotten occasion at the *Chronicle*, a newspaper sales operative transposed two crucial words when typing out a contents bill. This turned...

DOUBLE JOBS BLOW FOR TYNESIDE

into...

DOUBLE BLOW JOBS FOR TYNESIDE

Red faces all round, but the newspaper sales department did report exceptionally good sales in the city centre that night.

One of *Daily Express* Northern editor Tony Fowler's favourite reminders to his subs was: "No catchpennies!" By which he meant don't oversell the story on the news bill – it will disappoint the reader and could put them off buying the paper in future. I guess what Tony called a catchpenny back in the Eighties is now known universally as clickbait.

The line between a great news bill and a catchpenny can be a fine one. A *Coventry Evening Telegraph* sub wrote a bill highlighting a short story on the World News page about the trial of a South African who killed his wife and ate some of her remains in a home-made curry. The bill drove a sales lift of several hundred copies, prompting the newspaper sales manager to request a second helping of the story in the next day's edition. In my experience, curry is normally even better on the second day but on this occasion the sales boost wasn't repeated.

Contents bills are seen far less frequently nowadays, rendered largely redundant by the Internet, where every noteworthy news story is available almost as it happens, removing the opportunity for publishers to tease their readers into a purchase.

Another device which has all but disappeared from the sub-editing lexicon in recent years is the crosshead. This is a single, bold word which is slotted into the article by the sub to break up a slab of text and to encourage the reader to read on. Ideally, the chosen word should be impactful and eye-catching – Shock / Stunned / Bombshell, that kind of thing. This is all very well when the story is about a major news event but it can be more of a challenge when subbing a report from the local flower show.

A mischievous sub at the *Daily Express* claimed to have inserted four crossheads into a long feature article which, when taken together, read: Who. Reads. Crossheads. Anyway. The demise of the time-consuming crosshead is one aspect of the "good old days" that I suspect prompts few subs to shed a tear.

However, the very best bit of the sub's role is as important and relevant today as ever. There's nothing more satisfying to a sub than writing a good headline, particularly one that contains an element of wordplay or humour.

The Star's Charlie Bingham came up with a beauty when he was given an agency picture of Sheffield singer Joe Cocker, looking distinctly the worse for wear at an airport in Australia. The chief sub had earmarked the picture for Page One but there was precious little caption material and no news angle. And unless we wanted to invite a libel action, we couldn't say he was the worse for drink. Everyone on the subs' desk was scratching their head until Charlie passed a slip of copy paper over to the chief sub with his headline: "Cocker's Down Under". Which he was, in more ways than one.

Another headline that's up there with the best was penned by *Sunday Mail* editor Jim Wilson on a picture spread showing the bustling scenes at a big Scottish race meeting. Jim gave the lyrics of the old Stealers Wheel hit "Stuck in the Middle With You" a horseracing twist, turning "Clowns to the left of me, jokers to the right" into "Crowds to the left of me, jockeys to the right". Years later, that still makes me smile.

Staying with the horseracing theme, one of the better headlines I wrote never made it into print. In the early Eighties, the *Daily Express* was running a double-page spread on Ladies Day at Royal Ascot, where the ra-ra skirt (a layered mini-skirt) was the fashion choice *du jour*. The page designer had left a difficult shape for the headline – four decks with a tight count of just five characters per line. Everyone on the back and middle benches was asked to put their mind to it. Eventually, the deputy editor came up with a headline that didn't set the world alight but was deemed acceptable and, with time pressing, sent it to be typeset. A minute or two later, I volunteered:

A day

at the

ra-ra

races

The chief sub liked it but the deputy editor chose to stay with his effort. My two takeaways from this were (1) if you're going to upstage your boss, get your retaliation in first and (2) if I'm ever in his shoes, I mustn't let my ego deny someone their moment of glory. I hope I managed to stay true to that.

The most riveting racing-related headline I've ever seen was the work of Dave Phillips. Editor Clive Hutchby and I were interviewing him for a job as deputy chief sub at the *Chronicle & Echo*, in Northampton. At the time, Dave was working as a sub on the *Daily Sport*, which had carved a niche for itself by publishing eye-catching but increasingly outlandish stories. When I asked him: "What's the best headline you've ever written?" he shot straight back: "Lord Lucan seen riding missing Shergar".

For the benefit of younger readers, Lucan was a British aristocrat and gambler who disappeared after his children's nanny was found battered to death in his London flat. He has never been found. Shergar was a Derby-winning wonder-horse believed to have been kidnapped and killed by the IRA. He has never been found either. Like most of the stories in the *Sport*, it was a total fabrication but very funny. We gave him the job.

Every subs' desk worth its salt curates a Book of Boobs, capturing the worst howlers that make it through the production process and into print. The work of one sub, in particular, cropped up disproportionately in *The Sheffield Star*'s hall of shame. His speciality was the unintentionally inappropriate headline.

Working on the sports desk, he was asked to sub a report from the cricket at Bramall Lane, where the Indian touring team was playing Yorkshire. The morning session hadn't gone well for the tourists, who had lost several wickets. His headline: "Injuns in heap big trouble". He then tried his luck as a news sub, which didn't go any better. Subbing an inquest on a lorry driver who had died in a freak fall from his cab, he proffered the headline: "Oh heck, broken neck".

Sport provides an especially rich vein of gaffes, often as a result of the rush to get late-breaking match reports into print. In the late Seventies, the *Morning Telegraph* published a classic of the genre in a back-page picture caption, describing the moment a Sheffield United striker "thundered a shit against the bar".

I've heard it said by more than one chief sub that "a dirty mind makes for clean papers", by which they mean it's important to be alert to accidental double entendres. Obviously, a sub at the *TV Times* hadn't received that memo when they described Netherlands football captain Ruud Krol as the "record Dutch cap winner".

A headline that is part of newspaper folklore but is entirely apocryphal involved the acclaimed British explorer Vivian Fuchs, following the announcement that he was to lead an expedition to the South Pole. The story goes that a national newspaper editor saw a group of his subs tittering over a page proof, which contained the headline: "Fuchs off to polar ice". The furious editor said that couldn't possibly appear in print, and demanded it be changed to: "Fuchs off to Antarctica".

My former colleague Allan Rennie recalled a couple of gems by his subbing mentor Iain Scott in the *Stirling Observer*. His headline on a nature article discussing birds of prey: "All kestrel manoeuvres are a lark". And on an industrial tribunal involving a man who left a dead bird in his workmate's lunchbox: "Chirp butty".

But perhaps my all-time favourite headline appeared on the front page of the *Daily Telegraph*, on a report of an open-air concert in London's Hyde Park by Luciano Pavarotti, to celebrate his 30 years in opera. The heavens opened, drenching the 100,000-strong crowd, and a *Telegraph* sub summed it up perfectly with: "Rain in all arias".

The fear of repeating an embarrassing mistake can lead to some odd foibles. A colleague at the *Daily Express* told me that under no circumstances would his former editor at a local weekly allow the word "clock" to appear in his paper. It had to be "timepiece". Apparently, he had been scarred by his experience many years earlier when his report on a wedding informed readers that the bride had been presented with "an electric cock".

Sometimes, it's the juxtaposition of two perfectly good pieces of content that catches you out. In the late-Noughties, my commercial colleague Paul

House and I spent several months pitching for the Department of Health's Change 4 Life health and lifestyle campaign to appear in Trinity Mirror's titles. After a tortuous process and against stiff competition, we won the business, which was worth a substantial, six-figure sum.

What had given us the edge was our proposal to customise the content, with each of our titles producing their own local case studies to complement the centrally-produced, generic editorial. With the eyes of the Department for Health and its marketing and PR agencies on us, it was essential that the launch – a double-page editorial spread – appeared perfectly across 15 newspapers.

Determined to leave no margin for error, I arranged for the all of the editorial page proofs to be sent to me for checking; the 15 titles then made the corrections I'd highlighted and sent a second proof back to me for final sign-off. With every scrap of editorial content double-checked, it was all systems go!

Around half an hour after the papers were printed, the Department of Health's PR people were on the phone. They wanted to know why their expensive, high-profile anti-obesity campaign was positioned next to a full-colour advertisement for Marks & Spencer's cream cakes, with the headline "Go on, indulge yourself". It was a fair question.

Newsrooms are full of people who write for a living, so it's no surprise that words are often the journalist's weapon of choice. For my money, the benchmark for passive-aggressive wordsmithery was set by a chief sub-editor at the *Northern Echo*, who had a particularly fractious relationship with the assistant editor, one John Pifer. Essentially, they hated each other.

So on his final shift before leaving the company, the chief sub decided he would use the front page news-in-brief column to fire his parting shot. The *Echo*'s house style was for these single-paragraph stories to have no headline but for each one to begin with a bold, oversized capital letter, known in the trade as a drop cap. With painstaking care, the chief sub constructed the column so that the drop caps formed the acrostic:

F

U

C

K

P

I

F

E

R

Decades before the term had been invented, this was trolling of the highest calibre. I like to think that at least one or two of the *Northern Echo*'s readers noticed the message, appreciated the sub-editing skill involved, and managed not to choke on their corn flakes.

* * * *

One of my most curious experiences as a sub-editor involved a late-night encounter on a snowy moorland road with police hunting the Yorkshire Ripper.

From the day Wilma McCann's body was discovered on a playing field in Leeds to the night, more than five years later, when he was finally arrested in Sheffield, the Ripper cast a long, dark shadow across the North of England. Most of Peter Sutcliffe's gruesome attacks took place in West Yorkshire but on two occasions he crossed the Pennines to strike in Manchester.

His early victims were picked up in red light districts but, as the death toll rose, his attacks became bolder and more frequent. On Bonfire Night 1980, he attacked a 16-year-old girl in a Huddersfield street in the early evening. She survived because her boyfriend heard her screams and ran out of the house to give chase to the fleeing Sutcliffe. It was as close as the Ripper came to being caught in the act.

At the time of the Huddersfield attack, I was living near Holmfirth, just six miles to the south. I was working afternoon shifts in Manchester, which meant my wife was at home, alone, in the evenings. Call it an over-reaction, but there was a tangible fear that the Ripper might strike anywhere. So I took the precaution of upgrading our home security. In hindsight, a determined and resourceful serial killer probably wouldn't have been deterred by the flimsy,

5cm brass bolt I fitted to our half-glazed back door but, hey, it's the thought that counts.

Assistant Chief Constable George Oldfield, who had been drafted in to lead the police hunt, was focused – almost to the point of obsession – on the "I'm Jack" tapes. Recorded in a whispery Wearside accent, the hoax tapes had been sent in the post, addressed personally to Oldfield, by a man claiming to be the Ripper.

My car-share mate for the daily shift in Manchester was a former Sheffield colleague, who had landed a job at the *Express* around the same time as me and had bought a house just down the road. At around 2am on a winter's night, I was driving us back to Yorkshire when we were confronted by a police panda car blocking the otherwise deserted road. Two uniformed officers checked our ID and asked why we were on the road so late, where we'd been and where we were going. Despite the drama of the roadblock, the conversation was pretty low-key and they soon waved us on our way.

A couple of days later, two detectives arrived at my Sunderland-born workmate's home wanting to question him further. He told me afterwards that their tone was altogether more serious than in the moorland encounter and the interview far more detailed. When he had answered their questions, the policemen told him he would be discounted from their inquiries. As they were leaving, he said he assumed they had turned up as a result of the dead-of-night roadblock and that their colleagues had noted his Wearside accent. No, they said, we're here because your mother-in-law contacted us to say you might be the Ripper.

When it finally came, Sutcliffe's arrest in Sheffield unleashed a wave of overwhelming relief, not least among the senior police officers who had been hunting him for so long. The press conference they held the day after his arrest had an almost carnival atmosphere, with beaming smiles all round – even though the killer had been apprehended by a neighbouring force, and not by them.

But as more details emerged, the recriminations began. The photofit of the killer, based on descriptions given by survivors, bore an uncanny likeness to Sutcliffe; he was a lorry driver – one of the 'likely jobs' on the police list; his name had cropped up time and again as a potential suspect; he had been interviewed by the police NINE times; his workmates even referred to him as

The Ripper. But despite the mountain of circumstantial evidence pointing to him, West Yorkshire police had failed to join the dots.

Like his assistant George Oldfield, West Yorkshire Chief Constable Ronald Gregory had staked everything on the "I'm Jack" line of inquiry, which enabled Sutcliffe to remain at large for a further two years and commit five more murders. Two years after the Ripper's capture and following a damning inquiry into his force's handling of the hunt, Gregory retired. But he courted further controversy by selling his story to the *Daily Mail* for a reported £40,000. Relatives of Ripper victims branded it "blood money", and Home Secretary Leon Brittan called Gregory "deplorable".

Apparently deaf to criticism, he then accepted an invitation to undertake a lucrative lecture tour of the USA, on how to hunt down a serial killer. The monumental irony was not lost on the *Daily Mail*'s legendary cartoonist Mac. He produced a brilliantly scathing piece of work depicting Gregory in front of his American audience and telling them: "For the first five years, you look for a man with a Wearside accent …"

Chapter Six

Hot Metal Meets Cold Reality

Bob Newhart is a comedy genius. The American's 60-year career — spanning stand-up, TV, films and top-selling albums – was founded on his brilliant monologues, in which he takes absurd scenarios and, with deadpan delivery, draws them out for maximum satirical effect. In his best-known sketch, he plays an Elizabethan courtier who takes a phone call (stay with me here) from Sir Walter Raleigh, who is checking in from the Americas with news of his latest discovery. The script goes like this...

"What's to-bac-co, Walt? A leaf? What do you do with the leaves? Are you saying snuff, Walt? You take a pinch of it and you...stick it up your nose? And it makes you sneeze? I imagine it would, Walt, yeah.

"It has other uses...you can chew it...or stuff it in a pipe. Or you can shred the leaves...put it in a little piece of paper...roll it up...

"You don't have to tell me, Walt. You stick it in your ear, right?

"B-between your lips and then … **YOU SET FIRE TO IT**?"*

Newhart would have found the hot metal method of newspaper production to be fertile comic ground. To describe it as labyrinthine doesn't do this crackpot process any justice at all. In the mid-Seventies, as I was joining my first newspaper, the writing appeared to be on the wall for hot metal. Regional publishers had begun to replace it with computer-based phototypesetting systems, eventually leaving the nationals – where the print unions still had a stranglehold – as its last bastion.

Anyone under forty, brought up on desktop publishing, would struggle to comprehend how newspapers – one of the most time-sensitive products imaginable – could be built on such an arcane, ancient, labour-intensive system. For the uninitiated, the process went something like this:

It's funnier if you watch it on YouTube.

A reporter types a story (aka the copy), making sure to make a copy (aka a 'black') of the copy, using carbon paper*. The reporter hands their copy to the news desk, who review it and then give it to the chief sub-editor, who allocates the story a place in the paper. Then it goes to a sub-editor, who adds the typographical instructions (page number, type size etc), checks the copy for accuracy and grammar and writes the headline. The sub's work is checked by the revise sub-editor before being sent downstairs to the composing room via a Lamson tube.

Also used in banks and department stores, Lamson tubes comprised a rabbit warren of pipes running through the bowels of the building, using compressed air to fizz a cylindrical container, with the subbed story inside, to its next destination – in this case, the composing room.

On one memorable occasion during my time at The Star, the tube became blocked. An engineer arrived, inserted his arm and after a minute or two rummaging around, pulled out a of wad of paper that was stuck in the pipe. Among the yellowing sheets was a front-page splash from several years earlier. It's easy to imagine the telephone conversation on that day between the chief sub-editor and the composing room overseer:

Overseer: "Where's the f_____ splash?"

Chief sub: "I sent it half a f_____ hour ago."

O: "Well it's f_____ well not here!"

CS: "So what the f___ do you expect me to do?"

O: "Send the f_____ again. And make it f_____ quick!"

For younger readers, Wikipedia defines carbon paper as "a sheet of paper coated on one side with a layer of a loosely-bound dry ink or pigmented coating, bound with wax, used for making one or more copies simultaneously with the creation of an original document when using a typewriter or a ballpoint pen". A newsroom staple until the advent of word-processing and photocopying, carbon paper was messy, and the dust it produced was flammable and potentially toxic. I don't recall anyone telling us that at the time.

These days, newsrooms are quieter and more polite environments than in the macho hot metal era, when the industrial production process was matched by a liberal quantity of industrial language.

If the editorial part of the process sounds complicated, it is in the composing room where the really wacky stuff begins. The copy is picked out of the Lamson tube by an overseer and passed to a man (it was always a man) at a Linotype machine - a Heath Robinson contraption with a typewriter-style keyboard at the front, a system of clanking pulleys above and a pot of molten metal at the back. Invented by Ottmar Mergenthaler in 1886, the Linotype machine was revolutionary because it meant type could be set a whole line at a time (there's a clue in its name). Before Ottmar's stroke of genius, each single letter had to be painstakingly selected and assembled into words by hand.

The Linotype operator typesets the story according to the sub-editor's instructions. As he types out the story on his keyboard, the machine picks up a blank piece of metal, known as a slug, and injects blobs of metal into a mould, to form letters on the slug. When the whole story has been type-set, it is carried to the "stone" (a flat, metal area, not made of stone) where a compositor (aka a stone hand) assembles the stories on the page, working to a sketch drawn by a sub-editor. At this stage, the page is a mirror image of how the printed page will look, so the ability to read back to front comes in very handy.

A proof, known as a 'galley proof', is made, so a sub-editor (aka the stone sub) can check it for errors. Sorry, almost forgot - another proof of every story goes to the readers' department, where a load of men (again) check it, assisted by some other men called copyholders, who … hold the copy for the reader. The marked-up proof is sent back to the Linotype operators for any corrections to be done.

As typeset stories were carried around the composing room, it was inevitable that every now and then one would be dropped, causing the lines of type to be scattered all over the place. This is known as a printer's pie. The story is now a write-off and you have to go back to the start – a bit like snakes and ladders but much more annoying, especially when you're up against a deadline. In some newspaper offices, the production union's agreement with management stipulated that their members should be paid extra every time they had to re-set a story, which may help to explain why spillages of type were more frequent than one might expect.

When all the content for the page has been assembled, it is locked in place and an ink roller is run over it so another proof (a page proof) can be pulled, for final checking by the stone sub. On no account should a journalist touch the type at any stage of this laborious process, otherwise the Father of the Chapel (the newspaper unions' name for a shop steward) is likely to call a walk out, bringing the time-critical production of the paper to an immediate and potentially disastrous halt.

The stone sub marks any corrections on the page proof, which goes back to the Linotype operator to be re-set (again). When the corrections are in place and the page has been proofed (again), checked (again) and finally signed off, an impression of it is made on a flong (a spongey, flexible, green mat sort of thing), which reverses the page so the type is now the right way round.

The flong is then strapped to a semi-cylindrical piece of metal and the impression on the flong is transferred on to the metal, so the type is now raised (again) but is back to front (again).

The metal semi-cylinders are then strapped to the rotary press, ink is applied to the cylinders and paper (aka the web) is fed over it at high speed to print copies of the newspaper, which are then cut, bundled and distributed to newsagents across the circulation area.

This may sound ridiculous, and in many respects it was. It was also ridiculously successful; this method of production remained largely unchanged for 100 years. If you were to overlay the same product lifespan on to the motor industry, we would still have been driving around in Model T Fords at the beginning of the 21st Century.

As hot metal was gradually replaced by phototypesetting, the rows of clanking Linotype machines were replaced by quiet computer rooms, where banks of machines resembling supersized fridge-freezers but with less computing power than a Fitbit* spewed out yard upon yard of punched tape.

In the early Seventies, my father Eric was part of a three-man Sheffield Newspapers fact-finding team sent to the USA, to help choose a computerised phototypesetting system. When it was installed back in York Street, he took enormous pride in showing me how his new baby worked.

I made up the Fitbit comparison but it can't be far off.

Stories now arrived from the computer room as 'bromides' (photographic paper), the reverse side of which was waxed and stuck on to the page by a compositor, at a frame resembling an artist's easel. If the story was too long for the allotted space, the compositor used a scalpel to make cuts to it, following a sub-editor's instructions. The process became known by a generation of journalists and composing room staff as cut-and-paste or lick-and-stick. Every now and again a story would go missing, leaving a gap in the page and panic in the air. More often than not, it would be found stuck to the bottom of someone's shoe.

Compared with desktop publishing, there were still multiple steps in the phototypesetting process, and journalists were still forbidden from touching the "type". But it was a significant leap technologically and it paved the way for further, more radical change. These innovations took place rapidly across the regional press. Meanwhile the nationals, where the print unions retained a vice-like grip, ploughed on with hot metal for another ten years.

In the early Eighties, at the *Daily Express*, in Manchester, I was chatting to a newly-hired compositor, who had joined from a local jobbing printer's. In his mid-thirties, he was delighted to have landed this extremely well-paid job, which he was absolutely confident would see him through to a luxuriously-pensioned retirement. He'd been trying to get into national papers for some time, and had been rejected twice, by different publishers, before being accepted by the *Express*.

I listened slack-jawed as he explained that the recruitment process required all the national newspaper publishers to alert the National Graphical Association union of any vacancies, and that the union would put forward three candidates for interview. The NGA's shortlist was not based on the candidates' level of skill or relevant experience but simply by how long they had been on the list. If a candidate was rejected three times by the same publisher, the company had to provide the union with a written explanation for their decision. Little wonder the *Express*'s sharp-suited composing room managers – known dismissively as "floor walkers" by the compositors – were held in such low regard. The unions called all the shots.

More precisely, the print unions called all the shots. The NGA, NATSOPA and SOGAT derived their formidable bargaining power from a willingness to jeopardise newspaper production to achieve their aims, and the certainty that every member would fall into line with their instructions.

In contrast, the National Union of Journalists was hamstrung by two irresistible forces. Firstly, their members' instinctive desire to 'get the paper out'. And, secondly, the fact that journalists have passionately-held views. Lots of them. On just about everything. For NUJ officials, trying to herd this stroppy rabble of highly-opinionated cats towards effective industrial action was a thankless task.

This weakness was exposed when, in the run-up to Christmas 1978, the NUJ called all its regional press members out on strike in pursuit of an improved pay deal. On the first, chilly morning picketing *The Star*'s York Street offices, spirits were reasonably high. Editor David Flynn even arranged for a tray of tea and coffee to be sent out to us. But as the weeks rolled by, the goodwill on both sides ran out. The number of pickets dwindled and a miserable Christmas loomed. Every Thursday, we faced the ignominy of breaking off from picketing to queue at *The Star*'s back door to be handed a tax rebate of a few pounds – our only source of income, as the NUJ couldn't afford strike pay.

At the start of the six-week strike, Flynn and *Morning Telegraph* editor Michael Hides produced the papers almost single-handedly but eventually 12 journalists – nicknamed the Dirty Dozen – returned to work. And as the company's newsprint stock ran low, the management employed a professional strike-breaker to drive through the picket lines with fresh supplies. At that moment, it was clear the strike couldn't succeed.

Compared with their regional cousins, journalists at the *Express* couldn't grumble about their remuneration. I moved there for a 50 per cent pay rise – from £5,000 a year as a sub-editor in Sheffield to £7,500 at the *Express*, to do pretty much the same job. On top of that, every sub on the Express Newspapers payroll received a set telephone allowance of £36, for which no receipt was required.

During six years on the staff, I don't recall making or receiving a single work-related phone call. In the early Eighties, with inflation raging, our union officials argued for – and won – substantial pay increases; one year, our annual rise was 17 per cent.

The regional press didn't fare quite so well, causing the pay gap between regionals and nationals to grow even wider. This only became a problem if you chose to move back to the regionals, as I did in 1985, when I traded my £18,400 salary, guaranteed expenses and a 28-hour working week as an

Express sub-editor for £12,000 a year, a 50-hour week and responsibility for a team of seven, as features editor at the *Telegraph & Argus*, in Bradford.

Despite the generous pay and perks on offer in Manchester, every now and then someone couldn't resist pushing their snout a little too far into the trough. When a certain sports writer was struggling to conjure up his regular level of expenses, he was reduced to rooting around in the darkest corners of his desk drawer. To his delight, he found a crumpled restaurant receipt, which he submitted as evidence of his expense claim for lunch with a football manager. A couple of days later, the managing editor popped round to the sports reporter's desk and suggested he might "have another go" at his claim.

Sport guy: "What do you mean by that?"

Managing Editor: "The claim you've put in for lunch with XXXXX this month."

Sport guy: "Yeah, so what? I often take him out for lunch."

Managing editor: "But you might want to have another think about this one."

Sport guy (indignantly): "Are you accusing me of fiddling?" (The sports desk are all ears by now).

Managing editor: "I'm just saying you might want to drop it."

Sport guy (really wound up): "AND WHY SHOULD I?"

Managing editor: "Because this receipt doesn't have a VAT number on it, and I think you'll find the Chancellor of the Exchequer introduced VAT six years ago."

Sport guy: "Err ... OK.'"

Ultimately, Rupert Murdoch decided the bad old ways of print production couldn't be allowed to go on. In 1986, he delivered what would turn out to be the killer blow when he set up a new, computerised production plant at Wapping, and promptly dismissed his production workers. The unions called a strike, but after a year of often violent confrontation their resistance collapsed. For journalists who had seen at close quarters the deeply-ingrained

Spanish practices and day-to-day fraud that infected the production of our national newspapers, it was difficult to feel much sympathy.

Phototypesetting required a different and arguably more dexterous skill set than hot metal. But someone – OK, it was the print unions – decreed that the horny-handed men whose job had been to assemble lumps of lead-based alloy into newspaper pages would be naturals with a scalpel.

For those not familiar with it, a scalpel is a small, slim, incredibly sharp-bladed implement, used by surgeons to slice open human flesh – which is something the compositors at *The Star* would also achieve from time to time, accidentally slashing an innocent bystander, more often than not an unarmed sub-editor.

In fairness, many hot-metal compositors made the transition to cut-and-paste pretty well. But Bob didn't. In Bob's hands, a scalpel was transformed from a piece of inert metal into a writhing viper, liable to strike at any moment. As a stone sub, standing at his shoulder as he grappled chaotically with a page for the City edition, you quickly learned to be on permanent alert or you could expect to be saying hello to our friends in A&E.

As the print unions' grip was loosened bit by bit, it dawned on managements up and down the land that, generally speaking, a scalpel could be wielded more accurately and speedily by women. But not before a generation of sub-editors had gathered a fine collection of war wounds, courtesy of their colleagues in the National Graphical Association.

In the same way that canals enjoyed a brief spell as a new, disruptive technology, only to be rendered obsolete by the arrival of the railways, phototypesetting came and went within just 20 years, knocked off its perch by ever-slicker iterations of computerised production, which culminated in desktop publishing. By the mid-1990s, more than 200 years after the UK's first mass-circulation newspaper was launched, control of production was finally in the hands of journalists. (Cue maniacal laughter).

At the time, it seemed the future for journalists and journalism would be roses all the way. Sadly, this supposed golden age didn't last long.

Chapter Seven

Space Out, Spice In

Whenever I'm asked what's the best job you've ever had, it's no contest: Curry Correspondent of the *Bradford Telegraph & Argus*. When I joined the *T&A* as features editor, one of the things that leapt out at me was the lack of a weekly eating out column. This was an obvious gap so, having prised a modest budget out of editor Terry Quinn, our new Saturday feature was launched. It soon became popular with readers. It also made me quite popular among the reporters, who would never pass up the chance of a free meal in return for a 500-word review.

But after a few months, it struck me that we were missing a trick. We were working our way through the traditional restaurants, writing reviews in the time-honoured style, but the 100-plus Asian cafés in the borough were not getting a look-in. These hugely-popular, no-frills places began popping up in the late Fifties, after the first Pakistani immigrants had arrived in Bradford, to work in the woollen trade. Husbands came to Bradford alone and would share accommodation, saving as hard as they could until they could afford to bring over their families. The cafés fulfilled a dual role as a food station and also a social hub where the new arrivals could meet and chat. One of the very earliest, which was still trading during my time in the city, was known by everyone as the Karachi Social Club.

Over an after-work curry, chief sub-editor Clive Hutchby and I decided to launch the *T&A* Curry Guide, taking turns to write a fortnightly review. The cafés were so similar – basic furniture, similar menus, no alcohol, no cutlery – there was no point writing 500 words every time. So we decided on six paragraphs, and we would try to make it quirky and fun. Within a couple of months, our little feature had taken on a life of its own, with restaurant owners inviting us to visit, and readers urging us to try their favourites.

In one memorable piece, Clive was highly impressed by the latest place he had tried. He waxed lyrical about the knockout quality of the food, the wonderful flavours, the piping hot chapatis. His only less-than-glowing comment came in the final sentence, with the warning: "Don't use the toilets – they're grim."

One freezing winter's night, I visited a tiny place on a side street just off Manningham Lane, in the city's red light district. It was an end-of-terrace house, with the front room set up as the café. There were just three or four tables, with a teenage lad taking the orders. His dad was doing the cooking in the back. What puzzled me was the lack of any clue to what the place was called. There was no sign outside and the wall-mounted menu - one of those spell-it-yourself plastic boards with holes for the letters - didn't help either. I asked the lad for the name of the café. He frowned, and said he'd ask his dad. I watched as the two spoke. Dad thought for a minute and sent back the message: "Mansoor". I got the distinct feeling he made it up on the spot.

A few months later, I received a letter from a reader, telling us how much she and her husband enjoyed the Curry Guide. She explained that hubby Keith, a bus driver, was a keen curry cook, having learned some of his skills from his Asian workmates. Her letter ended with an invitation to Clive and me to visit their home and sample Keith's cooking. This was too good to miss.

We were welcomed warmly, looked after superbly and treated to a feast. With the couple's consent, I wrote a spoof review for the weekend edition, including a picture of their suburban bungalow home. I spent the next two weeks fielding calls from readers who were desperate for the phone number so they could make a booking.

The popularity of our feature spurred us to produce two stand-alone magazines, featuring the Best of the Curry Guide, both of which were sell-outs. A copy of the second volume found its way to the city's environmental health department, where it became the go-to reference book. Over the next few months several of our "Best in Bradford" award winners found themselves in court for hygiene offences.

* * * *

The *T&A* offices in Hall Ings had begun life as a woollen mill, built in Bradford's Victorian heyday. Externally, it looked magnificent; the futuristic, black-glass press hall that had been added to the Gothic-style mill building shouldn't have worked but somehow it did, beautifully. The old-meets-new look was a symbol of the times in newspapers. The mid-Eighties was a period of brisk evolution in the industry, when old-school traditions met new technology, with the two often running alongside each other for a time.

An old *T&A* hand told me that when the first computers were installed, the company still employed a caretaker, one of whose duties was to look after a pigeon loft on the roof. The pigeons' job was to bring news of goals and scorers from Bradford City's Valley Parade ground back to the office. Considering that their First World War forebears had to brave gunshots and artillery fire to ferry messages to and from the front, the *T&A* flying squad's half-mile hop across the city was a pretty cushy gig.

If the face the *T&A* presented to the world was a thing of eye-catching beauty, the building's interior was an entirely different matter. The editorial department – a collection of small, gloomy, high-windowed offices, painted a drab swimming-baths green with a generous top coat of nicotine stain – was particularly dreadful. After my final interview for the features editor role, editor Terry Quinn and his deputy Lawry Sear hesitated over whether to show me the features department, in case it put me off the job. Eventually, they gave me a quick peek. They weren't joking. To borrow my curry guide colleague's phrase, it was grim.

Glaswegian Quinn had been a surprise choice to edit the *T&A*. He had come from a small, weekly operation and was in his very early 30s – young to be handed control of a sizeable regional daily at that time. He told me he knew he was the outsider for the job, so he went into the interview with all guns blazing, advocating a no-stone-unturned overhaul of the title. He backed it up with a detailed plan and even some page designs, to show how he would modernise the appearance of the paper. His ideas impressed Westminster Press's editorial director Nick Herbert, who was already aware of Terry's get-things-done attitude. When the works manager at the weekly he edited had ignored his repeated requests to spruce up the dingy editorial department, Terry bought a can of paint and came in at the weekend to do the job himself.

The energy that had won him the *T&A* job was there for his editorial team to see, every day. He had hit the paper like a typhoon, shaking up the news agenda, demanding more of his subs, revamping the sports content, pushing the newspaper sales and marketing teams to raise their game. "Never accept second best" was his mantra. As for his management style, he practised a muscular form of motivation, which put me in mind of that big guy who beats out the rhythm to keep the galley slaves rowing.

Having returned from the bright lights of national papers to my roots in the regionals, I was under no illusions about the budgetary constraints I would have to work within. So it came as a surprise to discover that the *T&A* had its very own space correspondent, a luxury beyond even the most lavishly-financed national. It turned out our space correspondent was a British Gas engineer called Brian, who wrote the odd article about space or astronomy for us on the side. As well as the occasional *T&A* feature, he appeared every now and then on Saturday morning kids' TV.

During one of our chats, Brian told me about a big decision he was facing. The TV producers had asked him if he'd mind dressing up in a black cape with moons and stars on it, and a wizard-style hat. He was worried this wouldn't fit with his desire to be taken seriously as a space *aficionado*. I could see his dilemma. I advised him to go for the pointy hat and the cape. Brian knew quite a lot about his subject but his academic-style essays didn't fit in a local newspaper, so I decided to let them disappear quietly into the black hole of my desk drawer.

Quinn's non-stop modernisation of the paper continued at a blistering pace. Whenever we felt we could see light at the end of the tunnel, he would build a bit more tunnel; a new Saturday supplement here, a special nostalgia edition there. Everything was done with the aim of driving additional sales, to capture that rarest of beasts – an increase in our official 12-monthly circulation figure.

At the time, the Audit Bureau of Circulations rules stated that if the advertisements from a normal edition of the paper were also published in these special stand-alone editions, the sales could be included in the title's audited figures. In his relentless quest for a sales increase, Quinn was prepared to try anything. His most madcap wheeze was to resurrect – for one edition only – the long-dead *Yorkshire Observer*.

In the Eighties, no British newspapers were published on Good Friday. So Quinn decided we would be the exception. His plan was to produce an 84-page, one-off edition of the *Yorkshire Observer*, which had ceased publication many years earlier but was still registered as a newspaper and owned by Bradford & District Newspapers. It would be sold throughout Yorkshire – an area several times larger than the *T&A*'s normal footprint – to drive as many copy sales as possible and to maximise the PR opportunities across the county's broadcast media. It was an interesting little tale which got plenty of take-up on a quiet Bank Holiday weekend.

It fell primarily to Clive Hutchby, editorial artist Jon Binns and me to drive the content and design work. No extra resource, just do it alongside your day job, it'll be good fun, said Terry. And it was. It also gave me an opportunity to try my hand at a new skill.

We realised quite late in the day that we didn't have any horoscopes to slot into the puzzles page. We could have bought in a column from an agency but by this point it had become a badge of honour for us to produce the paper to the highest standard we could, at the lowest possible cost. So I sat at my terminal, gazed into my non-existent crystal ball and wrote "In the Stars", by Vanessa Mars.

Quinn liked a good editorial campaign, so long as it was "short, sharp and winnable". But, eschewing his own mantra for once, he threw the *T&A* wholeheartedly behind the nebulous and hard-to-measure *Bradford's Bouncing Back*, a spirited attempt to breathe new life and pride into a city with more than its share of post-industrial problems. He contacted the famous sons and daughters of Bradford, to enlist their support. Artist David Hockney – arguably the most famous living Bradfordian – responded from his home in Los Angeles with an idea of simple genius.

It was a piece of artwork entitled *A Bounce for Bradford*. Hockney drew a series of four separate pictures, each one depicting a bouncing ball, which he faxed* over to us. One was pink, one yellow, one cyan and one black – the four colours of full-colour printing. The first time the four balls would come together to form the completed piece of art was when they were printed on the *T&A*'s presses. *A Bounce for Bradford* was used as the cover of the *Bradford's Bouncing Back* launch supplement, and anyone who bought a copy could say they owned a Hockney original. Sort of.

While Terry would do almost anything to produce a newspaper sales lift, there was one occasion when even he drew the line. In a chat before the morning news conference, newspaper sales manager David Mothersdale revealed we were paying for a taxi to ferry copies of the paper to Morecambe, six days a week.

*Ask an old person.

Traditionally, Morecambe – jewel of the North West coast – had been a magnet for retired Bradfordians, who looked forward to spending their autumn years by the sea*. Of an evening, they liked nothing better than to leaf through a copy of the *T&A*, to keep in touch with events in their home city. And Bradford & District Newspapers was pleased to provide the long-distance delivery service.

The problem was that all the firm's vans were needed to distribute the paper across our patch of West Yorkshire, so a taxi driver was contracted to do one journey per day, a 177-mile round trip from Bradford to Morecambe and back, with copies of the *T&A* on the back seat. In the beginning, someone must have calculated that the additional sales made the cost of delivery worthwhile.

But over the years, as nature's pruning fork took its toll, the number of *T&A*-reading pensioners in the town dwindled. "So how many papers do we send there?" Quinn asked. Mothersdale replied, somewhat sheepishly: "Three." To this madness, a stop was quickly put.

But if sending three copies of the paper half-way across the country in the back of a taxi sounds unbelievable, it was nothing compared to a crackpot scheme to boost sales of the Cardiff-based *Western Mail*, told to me by Tony Hill, who was assistant managing director there at the time.

Looking to make an early impact, the newly-appointed managing director decided to focus on improving the *Mail*'s sales in rural North Wales. This was a perennially tough nut to crack, as road connections between the print plant in Cardiff and the north of the principality were poor, meaning there was insufficient time to get the papers to the local wholesaler for distribution. Trains, too, were a non-starter. But the new MD had a big idea, which he tasked Hill and the newspaper sales manager with putting into action. He was proposing to send the copies by light plane.

*Not too near the sea, though. When the tide's out, Morecambe Bay boasts the largest expanse of inter-tidal mudflats in the UK, and you'd need the Hubble space telescope to spot a trace of water.

Tony Hill: "But where will the plane land?"

Managing Director: "Oh, the plane doesn't land."

TH: "So what happens?"

MD: "We cover the bundle of papers in bubble-wrap and Sellotape. Then, when the plane gets to Lake Bala, it comes in low and slow and …"

TH: "Yes …"

MD: "…they chuck the bundle into the water. It might bounce a bit, like in The Dambusters, but the bubble wrap makes it float and stops the papers getting wet."

TH (incredulous): "And then what?"

MD: "There are two guys out on the lake, in a rowing boat."

TH: "A ro…"

MD: "They pick up the bundle and row back to the shore …"

TH: "But …"

MD (triumphantly): "…where we've got a fleet of vans waiting! The drivers split the papers between them and off they go to the newsagents. Any questions?"

This lunacy was planned to take place around 3 o'clock in the morning, with only torches and perhaps the odd moonbeam to light the way. I wish I could tell you they gave it a whirl but killjoy Hill and his newspaper sales pal managed to stall progress until, unforgivably, the idea died.

* * * *

With the main planks of his editorial plan bedded in, Quinn decided the time was right to refurbish the office. Not just a lick of paint this time but a full-scale gutting, taking out all the walls and turning the editorial rabbit warren into a properly-appointed, open-plan newsroom. Would we be moving out temporarily? No, everybody will squeeze into one half, we'll drop a plastic sheet across the middle and the builders can crack on in the other half. When the first half's done, we'll swap over. Simples!

The culmination of Quinn's editorship was the conversion of the *T&A* from broadsheet to tabloid format. His rationale was that he'd got the content of the paper in a condition he was happy with, so now was the time to go tabloid, with a marketing campaign to support the relaunch. He asked me – now his assistant editor – to lock myself away for a couple of weeks to design the tabloid. Normally, this would be done using dummy copy ("lorem ipsum…" etc) rather than the real thing. Creating enough real content to fill a whole dummy newspaper while still producing the real one is massively time consuming and requires a prodigious extra effort from the staff. So that, obviously, is what we did.

After a few tweaks to my first attempt, we were ready to print the dummy edition, which was then sent out for market-testing. When the research results came back, we were very happy. Current readers, lapsed readers and non-readers had all given the test edition a solid thumbs-up. One elderly reader told us she loved the *T&A* and bought it every day but she couldn't hold the broadsheet open because of her arthritis. "This little one's lovely, though."

The message coming back from all the focus groups was that the tabloid was easier to handle, easier to read – which became our relaunch slogan. The tabloid launch went well, and the handy-sized paper was warmly received by readers and advertisers. Copy sales enjoyed a small percentage boost for a couple of months before resuming the same slow but frustratingly steady downward trajectory of its broadsheet predecessor and every other newspaper in the UK.

Amid the office refurbishment and the tabloid relaunch, a new editorial publishing system was purchased, concentrating a little more control in the hands of the editorial team. The emergence of mobile technology meant that, for the first time, journalists could file their content from outside the office, directly into the editorial system.

It's fair to say that when it came to technology, *T&A* cricket correspondent David Warner wasn't a natural. An excellent journalist, he just couldn't get to grips with the equipment the company had provided for him to file his reports electronically from the Press box. After repeated training sessions, David finally mastered the process for attaching his laptop to a landline phone via a modem and he set off for Headingley, itching to show his new toys to his counterparts from the *Yorkshire Post* and the *Northern Echo*.

The first sign that all was not well was when the deadline for his lunchtime piece passed with no contact. A few minutes later, a flustered David rang in, asking to be put on to a copytaker to dictate his report in the traditional way. When he got back to the office, he spilled the beans. He had proudly displayed his new kit to the other cricket writers and gave them a teach-in on how it would connect him to the mothership ten miles away. They were mightily impressed, and David was revelling in his new-found place at the cutting edge of technology – until he tried to file his copy. To his horror, the ancient Bakelite phone in the Headingley Press box wouldn't fit into his state-of-the-art modem. His mates' tech-envy turned instantly to riotous laughter.

* * * *

My two, three-year spells at the *T&A* were punctuated by a six-month sojourn at the *Northampton Chronicle & Echo*, which was just long enough for me to become acquainted with negative equity and the current Mrs Benson. My Curry Guide chum Clive Hutchby, newly-appointed as editor in Northampton, asked me to join him as his deputy, and I accepted the offer. I was keen to have "deputy editor" on my CV and, after years on life support, my first marriage had breathed its last, so the timing was good.

The *Chronicle & Echo* newsdesk team took pride in coining witty nicknames for their reporting staff. Mark Green was "Veg"; quietly-spoken Mark Fielden was "Fieldmouse"; and James Meek, now a best-selling novelist, was "Mecon". My favourite was their sobriquet for Alizon (with a z) Jones. On her appointment as the paper's first environment correspondent Alizon was instantly renamed Ozone Jones.

Deputy news editor Peter "Bingo" Hall was a larger-than-life, country squire character, whose penetrating voice was a feature of the newsroom. On one legendary occasion, Hall picked up a call intended for the books editor. He asked the caller for his name several times but couldn't make sense of what he was hearing. "I'm sorry, what are you saying? Itchy Bits? ITCHY BITS?" Hall hollered across the room to news editor Jenny Oldfield: "Jen, there's a chap on here, says his name's Itchy Bits!" In fact, it was the celebrated Northamptonshire-born writer H.E. Bates.

The first inkling that my new job at the *Chronicle & Echo* might not last too long came 45 minutes into my first shift. I had barely taken off my coat when a call came through for me on the newsdesk phone. The caller wouldn't give his name. I picked up the call in a quiet corner of the office – it was Mike

Glover, deputy editor at the *T&A*. He wanted to let me know that editor Quinn was leaving, that he was going to apply for the job and – if he got it – would I come back to Bradford as his deputy? This was flattering and a little destabilising.

Wanting to keep my options open, I told Mike I would be interested and we agreed to speak again if he was appointed. I felt I couldn't allow the possibility of returning North stop me from committing fully to the *Chronicle & Echo*, so after three months in a hotel, I bought a flat in the town. Then, as surely as night follows day, Glover rang again to say he'd landed the *T&A* editorship. The next Saturday morning I arrived at his home in Shipley for my "interview", which involved a walk round Northcliffe woods with Mike and his collie Bonnie. When we got back, we drank coffee in his kitchen and I put pen to paper.

A few weeks later, I headed back to Bradford. I put my flat in Northampton up for sale, just as the property market crashed. It sold two years later, for tens of thousands less than I had paid, wiping out all of my equity. Professionally, I was climbing the ladder. Financially, I had slid down a huge snake. Romantically, things had taken a distinct turn for the better.

* * * *

News-wise, my second three-year spell at *T&A* certainly had its moments, the most memorable being the riots that followed the publication of Salman Rushdie's controversial book *The Satanic Verses*. The book provoked an international furore, with Muslim leaders denouncing it as blasphemous while those on the other side of the argument, mostly in the West, robustly defended Rushdie's right to free speech.

Iran's Ayatollah Khomeini declared a *fatwa* against Rushdie, forcing him into a life of lockdown, with a 24-hour armed guard. He and his wife Marianne Wiggins moved house 56 times – once every three days – in their efforts to remain safe. Despite Khomeini's death a few months later, the *fatwa* remained in place for nine years.

Tension had been building in Bradford and other UK towns and cities since the publication of *The Satanic Verses*. We received reports of skirmishes between white and Asian youths in the city's suburbs. This presented us with a delicate decision on how much prominence to give these events in the paper.

Acutely aware that overplaying it would pour fuel on the fire, Glover took a sensibly cautious approach. We had a duty to report the news but he decided we would do it in a neutral, matter-of-fact way, and not splash it on the front of the paper. After several consecutive nights of clashes, matters came to a head on Saturday afternoon. A large group from the Muslim community gathered outside the City Hall for an officially-sanctioned demonstration, where they were addressed by their leaders. As happened in other towns and cities, copies of *The Satanic Verses* were burned.

The day's edition of the *T&A* had been put to bed a couple of hours earlier and most of the staff had gone home. A couple of reporters were on duty at the demonstration. My girlfriend (now wife) Jo, who was working at the *Hull Daily Mail*, had come over for the weekend and we were getting ready to leave the office when things began to heat up outside. From the second-floor window, we could see a lot of police activity and heard the shouts of counter-demonstrators. Armed with a notebook each, we went out to help capture the action for Monday's paper.

As we reached City Hall, a wave of white youths came storming down the street, hurling half-bricks and stones. The Asian demonstrators were too far away to be struck but the police, who had formed a cordon across the road, bore the brunt. Each time the police gave chase, the rioters would disperse into the narrow city-centre side roads before re-grouping and swarming in again.

After an hour or so, the violence fizzled out and we returned to the office. I looked out of the window into Hall Ings and noticed a middle-aged white woman and an elderly Asian man standing at a bus stop. They were chatting amiably, and occasionally shook their heads, presumably in disbelief at the scenes that had taken place just around the corner.

* * * *

Over the course of any long career, there are bound to be highlights and lowlights. One of my lower lights occurred at the *Telegraph & Argus*, when I slept through the start of the first Gulf War.

Following Iraqi president Saddam Hussein's invasion of neighbouring Kuwait, forces from a coalition of 35 countries massed in Saudi Arabia, with the dual aim of averting a possible invasion by Saddam and to prepare for counter-offensive action. In mid-January 1991, the American-led coalition launched an aerial and naval bombardment. The next stage would be a ground attack, with coalition soldiers entering Kuwait to confront the Iraqi forces.

The UK media was on high alert as the coalition prepared to make their move. If they crossed into Kuwait at night, the Press Association would hit the phones to get Britain's editors out of bed. As soon as *T&A* editor Mike Glover had taken PA's call, he would ring me and between us we would alert the rest of the senior editorial team. They, in turn, would cascade the news to their staff, and bring them into the office to pull together a special edition.

On the crucial night, I forgot to switch off my answering machine, so when Glover called, he got a recorded message and not his deputy editor, who remained fast asleep, blissfully unaware that the nation's Press was being summoned to battle stations.

The next morning, feeling fully refreshed, I switched on the radio to hear the invasion had begun. With my heart in my mouth, I ran downstairs and saw the answering machine flashing red. An hour later, when I finally slunk, shamefaced, into the newsroom, it's fair to say Glover wasn't desperately pleased. Meanwhile, my colleagues were keen to inquire if I'd had a good night's sleep, enjoyed a relaxing breakfast, heard anything interesting on the morning news …

Chapter Eight

Tragedy in the Afternoon

I had been at the T&A two months when fire tore through a stand at Bradford City's Valley Parade stadium, causing the death of 56 fans. It was the biggest peacetime event to hit the city and the biggest news story of my career.

On the last day of the league football season, Grandstand presenter Des Lynam was in a playful, end-of-term mood. As he gave an update on scores from up and down the country, he rounded off with: '...and at Valley Parade, there are even reports of a fire!' Indeed, this was meant to be a joyous day for Bradford City supporters, who had packed into the ground to see their team proudly parade the Third Division trophy before their final game, against Lincoln City. But as the scale of one of Britain's worst sporting tragedies began to unfold, Lynam's mood became altogether more sombre.

He reported that the main stand was ablaze, and it was believed a number of people had lost their lives. By teatime, the death toll stood at around a dozen. Over the course of Sunday and Monday, with each update from the police, that number went up. Ultimately, 56 people lost their lives and at least 256 more were injured. At one stage, the death toll was reduced by one, and when asked for the reason the police told a *T&A* reporter that, such was the ferocity of the blaze at the back of the wooden stand, a roll of burnt plastic sheeting had been mistakenly counted as a human body.

David Gledhill, who later became editor of the *Bath Chronicle*, was a *T&A* reporter at the time of the fire. Here are his recollections:

Saturday, May 11, 1985, the day everything changed for the people of Bradford and everyone at the Telegraph & Argus. Inevitably, we all knew someone – relatives, friends, work colleagues – touched by the terrible fire at Valley Parade on what should have been an afternoon of celebration for Bradford City fans. Less than an hour earlier the club been presented with the Football League Third Division Trophy.

Our chief photographer, Dennis Flatt, captured the whole thing from the first wisp of smoke to the all-consuming inferno that followed just a few minutes later – many pictures that were either only used once or not at all. In just four minutes, the stand was engulfed and in the mass panic that followed some fans escaped on to the pitch, but those that opted to climb up and out of the back of the stand found the doors locked and many were burned to death at the turnstiles.

The T&A became the focus not just for the coverage of the tragedy but it also reflected the mood of the city and supported the shocked population in their grief. In the weeks that followed we were with people at church memorial services, we were with them at gravesides and we were with them as they recovered from often horrific injuries in hospital. We were also at the forefront of a huge fundraising campaign that sought to ease the financial burden of so many families who had lost loved ones.

We didn't just report the story, we were part of the story, a story that had ripped through the community that we were at the heart of. We lived every moment of it and were often overwhelmed by the emotion. And despite what is often levelled at newspapers in times of crisis, we got it right, because we knew our readers and felt their pain.'

When I arrived at the office on the morning after the fire, Dennis Flatt's prints – hundreds of them – were laid out on deputy editor Lawry Sear's desk. Lawry was sorting them into those which were usable and those which it would never be appropriate to publish. It was a graphic pictorial record of one of Britain's worst sporting disasters. The phones were ringing non-stop with calls from newspapers and news agencies around the world, wanting pictures from the fire. All enquiries were directed to Lawry, to keep control of the process and to take the weight off a hard-pressed newsdesk.

Editor Terry Quinn decided that all proceeds from the sale of the pictures would go to the disaster fund in aid of the victims and their families, and Lawry was relentless in making every penny he could to help ease their suffering. He went on to have a glittering career, as editor of the *Eastern Daily Press* and managing editor at both the *Daily Mail* and the *Daily Telegraph*. But that weekend in Bradford may just have been Lawry Sear's finest hour.

As features editor, my job for the Monday edition was to put together a new leader page focusing on the fire. There wasn't a lot that could be said from the features point of view at this stage, other than general background about the stadium and a recounting of previous sporting disasters. The event itself was so recent and raw that news reporting was the main focus. In truth,

I was a bit-part player as the reporters continued to work flat out to tell the many stories of human tragedy and bravery that had played out in and around the stadium on that sunny May afternoon.

For weeks afterwards, Bradford was eerily quiet, a city in a state of shock. The *T&A* reporting team continued to dig out news stories and then attention began to turn to the cause of the fire and who should be held responsible.

As is often the case, a combination of factors came together to produce tragic consequences. The cause of the fire was a single cigarette, discarded by a fan, which fell through the floorboards on to a huge pile of tinder-dry rubbish that had built up beneath the stand over many years. In less than four minutes, the wooden structure was engulfed in flames, fanned by a strong wind. Intense heat from the burning roof set fire to the clothing of fans below. Some ran on to the pitch, their hair and clothes ablaze.

Later, it was revealed that the stand had been condemned and was due to be demolished just two days after the fire. The courts decided the football club was two-thirds responsible for the tragedy, finding that – despite repeated warnings – it gave '"no or very little thought to fire precautions". The city council was deemed to be one-third responsible.

A year or so later, stories began to surface of police officers leaving the force early. These were the first of a growing number of cases of the recently-discovered condition of post-traumatic stress disorder among emergency services staff, caused by their involvement on the day of the fire and in the aftermath.

The *T&A* editorial team responded to this terrible event in the most magnificent way, all of them understanding the profound impact the fire would have on the city. For most of the young reporters, this was the biggest story they would ever cover. Many of the staff were born and raised in the city or the surrounding area. Some were at the game and witnessed the disaster at first hand.

When a serious incident hits their community, a local reporter's instinctive response is to click into professional mode, to seek out the facts and tell the story. More than 30 years later, I saw the same reaction from staff at the *Manchester Evening News* after the Manchester Arena bombing. To say the coverage of both these awful tragedies was outstanding does not begin to do the newspapers justice. In both cases, the coverage was comprehensive, sensitive and finely detailed, and the reporters sought answers to many searching questions.

Above all, they showed enormous compassion, born of being local. And, as my colleague David Gledhill described, long after the rest of the press had moved on, the local paper stuck with the story and played a central role in bringing the city together and helping it to heal.

A third shining example of the local newspaper playing an outstanding role on behalf of its community following a hugely traumatising event was the *Liverpool Echo*'s superb campaign on behalf of the 96 victims and families of the Hillsborough tragedy – the torch being carried with huge determination by three different *Echo* editors. For 27 years, when the rest of the world didn't seem to care, the *Echo* was unswerving in its efforts to achieve justice for the city and its people. Don't let anyone tell you that local papers are all about cats stuck in trees.

* * * *

One of the fundraising events following the Bradford City fire was a football match at Halifax Town's ground, The Shay, between an All Stars XI and the West Yorkshire Media. It gave me the unforgettable joy of being on the same pitch as an England World Cup winner and my boyhood footballing hero.

The All Stars were ancient, but they were proper players. They included former Manchester United and Ireland goalkeeper Paddy Roache, former Leeds United and England captain Trevor Cherry, Scottish international Arthur Graham (who played as though it was a cup final), Huddersfield Town legend Frank Worthington, World Cup winner Nobby Stiles (who, without his glasses, could barely see the pitch let alone the ball), and former Sheffield Wednesday and Scotland maestro Jim McCalliog, who was now running a pub in Halifax.

The day before the game, *BBC Look North* ran a teaser piece. Shot from behind the goal, it showed a 'mystery keeper' saving shots from Worthington. It ended with the big reveal – the goalie was Look North presenter Harry Gration, who turned to the camera and urged viewers to turn up to the match to support the fundraising effort.

When the camera stopped rolling, Worthington put his arm around Bradford-born Gration and said: "You know, Harry, there'll be a time in the match when I'll get the ball on the edge of the penalty area. I'll put my foot on it, look at you, and curl a shot into the top corner. And you'll look a right ****." Sure enough, midway through the first half Frank stood and delivered. After Harry picked the ball out of the net, he turned to see a smiling Worthington giving him a cheery wave before trotting back to the half-way line.

Meanwhile, in the midfield engine room, I came face to face with my hero McCalliog. With more enthusiasm than skill, I hurtled into a 50-50 challenge with the lightly-built Scot, crashing into his chest and laying him flat on his back with the wind knocked out of him. I was mortified. I apologised profusely and offered him my hand to pull him back to his feet. Eyeing me from his position on the turf, Jim mustered enough breath for a succinct 'F*** off!' The first half ended with the All Stars leading 4-0. A goal soon after the restart gave the Media XI hopes of a comeback victory, but in the end we were narrowly edged out.

RESULT: All Stars XI 17 (seventeen), West Yorks Media XI 4

Chapter Nine

The Family Way

I f there was a competition to find the quintessential family newspaper, the *Coventry Telegraph* would have been my odds-on favourite. The paper was founded in 1891 by William Isaac Iliffe as the *Midland Daily Telegraph*, a four-page broadsheet selling for half an old penny. For the next 96 years of its life, the *Cov Tel* was owned by a succession of Iliffes, who took great pride in William's creation.

In the post-war period, Coventry was rebuilt, physically and economically, by young, skilled people attracted to the city by the work opportunities on offer. Many came from Ireland, Scotland and the North East of England to make the city their home, and to start families. As they settled in, they turned to the *Telegraph* for their daily news. So, for good business reasons, the paper was aimed four-square at a family audience.

As an employee, the *Telegraph* had a strong family feel, too. In the early Nineties, when I edited the paper, it wasn't unusual for three generations of the same family to be working there. While serving the UK's eleventh-largest city, the *Cov Tel* retained a distinctly homely vibe.

When I arrived in Coventry, in April 1991, the *Evening Telegraph*'s centenary celebrations were in full swing. This presented me with a great opportunity to meet many of the key players in the city and to understand from the outset the enormous affection in which the *Telegraph* was held. A highlight of the centenary year was a service of thanksgiving at Coventry Cathedral, led by the Bishop of Coventry and attended by the great and the good of the city.

One memorable moment involved a *Cov Tel* delivery van being driven up the nave of Sir Basil Spence's iconic masterpiece and dropping off a bundle of newspapers, for distribution among the congregation. At the swanky lunch that followed, Jo was seated next to the paper's former owner, the octogenarian Lord Iliffe. He opened the conversation with a brusque: "Who are you?" Jo replied that she was the editor's girlfriend. "What?" said his lordship, "Editors have girlfriends nowadays, do they?" I think you could say he was "old school".

Although the Iliffes had sold the paper four years earlier to the American publisher Ralph Ingersoll, the family's many years of ownership still ran through the veins of the business, which retained a number of quaint reminders of the past. On the third floor of the main offices in Corporation Street, there was a fully-equipped flat, installed during the Iliffes' reign, for their use when they were visiting the *Telegraph* from their family seat in Berkshire. The flat, it is worth noting, boasted a wine loft. The Iliffes were remembered fondly by long-serving staff as excellent employers. As well as an in-house social club and a subsidised canteen, Coventry Newspapers owned a sports ground, with its own pavilion, for the benefit of staff.

There was even a company doctor – an avuncular Scottish chap named Dr Keenan, who held a surgery at our offices every other Tuesday morning. He also organised annual medical check-ups for the senior executives. I looked forward to these examinations, as they provided the evidence that I was the fittest member of the management team – something I could dine out on for the next 12 months. However, my smugness rebounded on me one year when the good doctor dropped in to give me my test results.

Expecting the usual thumbs up and a few flattering comments, I was taken aback when he began: "Well, I never thought it would be you, of all people ..." He went on to tell me my white blood cell count was low and he would have to refer me to hospital for tests. This gave my hypochondria an opportunity to stretch its legs. Which it did. Like Usain Bolt in the Olympic 100 metres final. By the time I got home, I was convinced I was going to die. Me, with a new baby and a new Rover 800*. I had everything to live for.

Two weeks later, Doc Keenan dropped by again with my follow-up results. Everything was A-OK. Fine and dandy. Nothing to worry about. Clean bill of health. I was delighted, of course, but this was quite the turnaround from his Grim Reaper shtick of a fortnight earlier. What could have caused the low reading, I wondered? "Have you had a cold lately?" Yes I had, a week or two before the tests. "Oh, that was probably it, then." It was the only time in my life I've felt the urge to kiss someone and strangle them at the same time.

*It was metallic red but the Rover brochure described the colour as "pearlescent nightfire". Jeez.

Ingersoll had abandoned the U.S. newspaper market after his company defaulted on an interest payment. He then focused on the papers he owned in the West Midlands and Ireland, which were overseen for him by a handful of American directors. They had a flinty approach to management, which to those brought up on the benevolence of the Iliffes was culturally alien.

My first encounter with an Ingersoll lieutenant came after Coventry managing director Ernest Petrie had verbally offered me the *Cov Tel* editorship. Before Ernest and I were allowed to seal the deal, group editorial director Chazy Dowaliby wanted to give me the once-over. "Nothing formal, just a chat," Ernest assured me.

Arriving for my appointment in the directors' suite at the *Birmingham Post & Mail*'s offices, in Colmore Circus, I was met by a pleasant woman in a classic black-and-white waitress outfit. She looked like she'd stepped straight out of Lyons Corner House, circa 1930. She showed me in and introduced me to Chazy. Our "chat" lasted three hours, and included a half-time break for profiteroles and a pot of tea, served by the Lyons lady.

The American directors had strong views on how to produce good newspapers, but they didn't always translate well into the UK environment. I took my lead from Ernest Petrie, whose long career as a Thomson Newspapers executive had made him expert in handling this type of situation. In short, listen, nod thoughtfully, then quietly go about doing it your own way.

To everyone's surprise, not long after he had invested heavily in new, colour presses, Ingersoll put his Midlands titles up for sale. For a few weeks, a parade of suits representing potential buyers including European publishers and UK venture capitalists stalked our corridors, making notes and sizing up the business. Having been in post for just a few months, I found this a little unnerving.

Rumours abounded about who our new owners would be, but as potential suitors dropped out it became a shoot-out between the American directors, who were Ingersoll's favoured purchasers, and the British management team, led by Birmingham-based CEO Chris Oakley and including Coventry managing director Petrie. As the rivals slugged it out, the staff were advised to remain strictly neutral but there was no doubt about our desired outcome – we were rooting for the six Brits.

Eventually, the Americans had to admit defeat and Oakley had the prize, for £125 million. This seemed a huge figure, and some commentators were quick to express the view that he had overpaid. The following September, the UK Government was forced to withdraw the Pound from the European Exchange Rate mechanism, triggering the chaos of Black Wednesday. For a brief period, interest rates rocketed from an already-chunky 10 per cent to an eye-watering 15 per cent, and Oakley's phone was hot from industry contacts wanting to commiserate with him, as surely this would see his buyout go bust.

I've no doubt that some of the callers, envious of Oakley's buccaneering deal, wanted to see him fall. But the financing arrangements he had put in place with his banks included a cap on interest charges, so he and the MBO* team knew they could ride out the storm.

The 18 months following the management buyout were a joy. The chain of command at the newly-renamed Midland Independent Newspapers was beautifully short – if I needed a decision, I could nip up two flights of stairs and get my answer directly from one of the men who owned the company. Oakley also made the smart move of inviting Robert Iliffe to join the Coventry board, creating a strong link between the company's heritage and the new owners.

Management meetings in Coventry would take place in the third-floor boardroom, which was also well used for entertaining. Managing director Petrie would regularly invite significant advertisers and the city's decision makers for a delicious lunch, cooked on the premises, to help cement our key external relationships.

Nowadays, the idea of these leisurely, three-course business bunfights may seem excessive but until the turn of the Millennium it was common practice in the regional press. In fact, compared with the previous generation, belts had been tightened significantly. In the early Seventies, when my father Eric was promoted to the Sheffield Newspapers management team, managing director Tom Watson expected all his senior men (the glass ceiling was still firmly intact at this point) to assemble for a three-course boardroom lunch, with alcohol, every weekday.

*Oakley ensured his MBO would be remembered through the generations by naming his son, born shortly after the buyout, Maxwell Barnaby Oakley.

Editor Colin Brannigan decided he couldn't justify an hour and a half away from his desk at a crucial time of day, so he introduced an alternative – a working, sandwich lunch in his office with his editorial department heads. This didn't go down too well with Mr Watson but from a health perspective, Brannigan's breakaway was probably a wise move; after a couple of years of enforced dining, my increasingly corpulent father sent his work suits to a local seamstress, with an instruction to ease out the waistbands by several inches.

The Coventry boardroom was beautifully appointed, boasting an antique sideboard, a huge dining table, and 16 dining chairs, upholstered in a striking, light-blue fabric. The Iliffes had retained ownership of the furniture when they sold the business to Ingersoll but, in a generous gesture, allowed it to remain in the *Telegraph* boardroom. Sadly, the family's relationship with Oakley eventually turned sour and Robert Iliffe took his bat home – along with his sideboard and dining chairs.

Being a trained observer, I spotted at our next board meeting that the sumptuous blue seating had been replaced by a rather more functional style, constructed of tubular steel and orange plastic. Our jaws hit the floor when we were told the sideboard was supposedly worth half a million pounds and the chairs a further three-quarters of a million. Had we known that, I wonder if we would still have danced on them at the previous year's executive Christmas party?

* * * *

The great media rivalry in the Midlands at this time was between the *Birmingham Post & Mail* and the *Wolverhampton Express & Star*, Britain's biggest-selling regional daily. Shortly after Oakley's buyout, I was among a group of Birmingham and Coventry executives invited to a dinner hosted by the *Express & Star* management team in their boardroom. It was a convivial get-together, with the *Express & Star* team having the occasional good-natured dig about our newspaper circulation compared with theirs and the gut-busting size of the buyout team's "mortgage".

Oakley took their jibes in good spirit but as the evening drew to a close, he pointed to a large painting that dominated the boardroom. It was a scene from the African plains with, in the foreground, a family of big cats gathered on top of a mound. Oakley looked at it admiringly and said: "I always think that painting sums up your business so well. A bunch of cheaters sitting on a dung heap." Game, set and match to the visitors.

Our 18-month post-buyout golden period came to an end when the team's focus switched towards the impending Stock Market flotation of MIN. While their absence made life a bit more difficult for the rest of the executives in Coventry and Birmingham, it was entirely understandable. The six-man team had put a serious amount of their own money (not to mention their homes) on the line, and flotation had always been their ultimate goal.

The float was a success, and the team and their backers had their reward. A few years later Oakley and his team repeated their coup by acquiring United Newspapers' titles in Yorkshire and Lancashire and selling them to Johnston Press two years later for £560 million, making another significant profit.

A year or two after the Midlands buyout, Oakley gave a hugely entertaining speech at the Society of Editors' annual conference, revealing the inside story of the Ingersoll deal, and describing various alleged shenanigans by the competing bidders. It brought the house down. It also brought him a libel writ.

* * * *

By the time I began my career, most cities in the UK were served by a single local newspaper. In places where there were two papers - Sheffield, Liverpool and Birmingham, for example - they were almost always morning and evening stablemates, based in the same office and published by the same company. In Coventry, direct competition for print readers just didn't exist. So it was with great excitement, and a dash of anxiety, that the *Evening Telegraph* found itself locked in a three-way newspaper war.

Hostilities commenced early in 1992, after the publisher of the *Nuneaton Evening Tribune* decided to turn the title into a weekly. Despite being the largest town in Warwickshire, Nuneaton is just eight miles north of the city of Coventry. With a Coventry postcode, the town is fated to live in its larger neighbour's shadow. In terms of newspaper publishing, this made commercial life increasingly tough for the *Tribune*, particularly at times when the economy took a dip. After 97 years as a daily, the owners calculated that their business model was running out of road, and that switching to weekly publication offered a better long-term prospect.

In those days, there was an unwritten law in regional publishing that you don't encroach on your neighbour's patch, so it came as a surprise to the *Trib* when the *Cov Tel* scooped up three of their best reporters and launched a full-blown edition into the town. We were building from a strong base – we already had three reporters there, producing a reasonable local news service. But we reasoned that by providing more local news, sport and advertising, and leveraging our established distribution operation, we could fill the gap left by the *Tribune*. We calculated that if we could pick up a third of their readers, we would break even.

Irritatingly, the *Leicester Mercury* spotted the same opportunity, and they too launched an edition into Nuneaton. Theirs was more of a guerrilla assault. The *Mercury* was starting from cold, having had no previous presence in the town, and they were raiding from east of the A5, which marks the border between Leicestershire and Warwickshire. Their Nuneaton edition was more lightly resourced, with much of the coverage done from Leicester. Nevertheless, the *Mercury* was a big paper, with a well-staffed newsroom and, as part of the Northcliffe regional newspaper empire, they had heavyweight backing.

Added to that, the editor was Alex Leys, one of the leading names in regional publishing. A feisty Scot who I had known since my days as a trainee in Chesterfield, Leys was not one to back away from a scrap. And there was an extra twist – my partner Jo was working at the *Mercury* as a sub-editor, which gave Leys a golden opportunity to feed propaganda and disinformation over the county border and into our living room every evening.

No sooner had the *Telegraph* and the *Mercury* launched our new editions than a third combatant entered the fray. A handful of staff who had been made redundant by the *Tribune* decided to launch a new title – the *Nuneaton Evening News* – with the financial backing of a local businessman. So, while even London (population nine million) had tried and failed to sustain two daily newspapers, Nuneaton (pop. 86,000) was now served by three. What a time for news-hungry Nuneatonians to be alive.

The interest of BBC West Midlands was piqued by the Nuneaton Newspaper War, and they decided to run a feature on their nightly regional TV news magazine. Interviewed in the *Cov Tel* car park, I was asked to respond to accusations that the big-city bullies from Coventry had been tearing down news bills posted by staff from the plucky little newcomer, the *Evening News*. I told the reporter that while I had no knowledge of the specific allegation, (a) competition was a good thing, (b) the people of Nuneaton were enjoying the best news service anywhere in Britain, and (c) it was all good, clean fun.

And all the while I was wishing the other two would just clear off and leave us to feast on the *Tribune*'s corpse.

The Nuneaton Newspaper War was great fun while it lasted, but it didn't last long. After several months struggling to establish a sustainable foothold, the *Leicester Mercury* made a slow withdrawal (slow, so we couldn't crow about having beaten them). Over time, sales of the *Cov Tel*'s Nuneaton edition slowly shrank. Eventually, the financial pressure on the industry increased to the point where the *Cov Tel* – in common with almost all regional papers – had no option but to produce just one edition per day.

The *Evening News* was relaunched, somewhat curiously, as the *Heartland Evening News* before eventually becoming the weekly *Nuneaton News*. From its origins as an independent start-up, the *News* is now owned by Reach plc, the UK's biggest news publisher. Reach also owns the *Coventry Telegraph*, the *Leicester Mercury* and the *Nuneaton Tribune* (now a section of its *CoventryLive* web site).

Chapter Ten

An Audience with an Armed Robber

A s he sat across the desk from me, wearing a pale-grey suit jacket and horn-rimmed spectacles, I couldn't help thinking that Mick Bromell didn't look like your typical armed robber.

In the late Eighties and early Nineties, Bromell was Coventry's most notorious criminal, with a string of convictions and considerable jail time behind him. Over the years, the *Evening Telegraph* had published numerous articles documenting his crimes. Now here he was in the editor's office. He was angry, and he wanted to strike a deal.

Bromell had turned up at our Corporation Street HQ unannounced and unexpected. A normally bright-and-breezy member of the reception staff could barely get the words out as she squeaked down the phone: "There's a Mr Michael Bromell to see you." We both knew it was THE Mr Michael Bromell. While the journalist in me was intrigued, the coward in me was distinctly nervous. I asked the receptionist to send him up in the lift.

Despite his fearsome reputation, Bromell was softly spoken, almost shy. Our meeting, which can't have lasted more than 20 minutes, sparked a chain of events that climaxed a few months later in two dramatic days in court.

* * * *

I had joined the *Coventry Evening Telegraph* around a year before Bromell's visit. Two clear memories have stayed with me from my first day in my new job: firstly, the euphoria of sitting in the editor's chair and thinking "I've finally made it"; secondly, the heart-sinking moment when my deputy editor Roger Monkman said : "There's a nasty-looking legal you should know about ..."

Monkman outlined that two detective constables in the West Midlands Serious Crime Squad were suing us – along with a Who's Who of the British media – for libel. They had the financial backing of their union, the Police Federation.

The two officers had been accused of stealing interview notes in a case involving Michael Bromell but when the Director of Public Prosecutions decided they should not be prosecuted, they launched a raft of libel actions. Among those in their sights were the *BBC*, *The Times*, the *Daily Telegraph*, *The Guardian* ... and the *Coventry Evening Telegraph*. All of us had run stories alleging that two members of the Serious Crime Squad had tampered with evidence.

For several months, our case didn't move along much as the Police Federation's legal team concentrated on negotiating out-of-court settlements with the national newspapers and broadcasters. Our libel lawyer, Nick Alway, of Oswald Hickson, would ring me every now and again with the news that another publisher had settled. As each domino fell, the pressure on the rest cranked up a notch. Eventually, the *Cov Tel* – by far the smallest and most tightly resourced of the defendants – was the last one standing.

Nick and I felt we had a strong case and we were surprised that the bigger fish were capitulating so easily. But the spectre of the Police Federation loomed large. They had cavernously-deep pockets, and everyone in the media knew that when it came to pressing their members' interests, they never backed off.

So we had a decision to make. Or rather Chris Oakley, our chief executive, did. I travelled to the company HQ in Birmingham to talk him through the case and to ask him to spend a sizeable chunk of money to obtain an opinion from a Queen's Counsel. To put it in context, the sum I was asking for would have bought a family car or paid a reporter's wages for several months.

The first time I had encountered Oakley was around 14 years earlier, at the Reubens Hotel, in Central London. Aged 23, I had just made the switch from reporting to subediting and was despatched to London to attend a course to accelerate my learning.

Oakley, then assistant editor of the *Yorkshire Post*, was a guest speaker. The three highlights of my week in the capital were: a visit to the cinema to see *2001: A Space Odyssey*; sinking numerous pints of Young's and Fuller's ales at a variety of backstreet pubs; and Oakley's presentation about headline writing, which was funny, full of useful tips and delivered in an effortless style. He was the kind of journalist I wanted to be.

After the *Yorkshire Post*, Oakley had built a reputation as a fearless, campaigning editor, first at the *Lancashire Evening Post* and then at the *Liverpool Echo*, where he took on the hard-left Militant Tendency, who controlled the city council. Now, as CEO of the Birmingham and Coventry titles, he was one of the biggest beasts in the regional newspaper industry. And here was I, a newbie editor, trying to persuade him to throw (even more) money at a case the rest of the media world had given up on.

After taking a deep breath, I explained the background, told him why we thought we had a good case and why he should open the company cheque book. He listened attentively, asked me two or three questions, paused for a moment and then said: "I think we should do it". He shook my hand, wished me luck and asked me to let him know how we got on.

There was no guarantee that the money I'd asked for would get us anywhere but the CEO had listened and backed my judgement when it would have been far easier to take the pragmatic decision and cave in. I was over the moon. And it was next stop London, for a meeting with the Silk.

* * * *

Nick Alway and I sat in a garret office in the Inns of Court, being baby-sat by a junior barrister as we awaited the arrival of Desmond Browne QC. The walls were a drab cream and every surface was loaded with pink-ribboned legal files. It was distinctly pokey. Browne was a rock-star lawyer, specialising in defamation cases. He would later represent A-list clients including Naomi Campbell, Elton John and Michael Douglas, before going on to become Chairman of the Bar.

Browne made his entrance, took a seat and listened intently as the case was outlined to him. He was mightily impressive, asking the occasional, very precise question, then summarising the points of law before finally giving us his opinion on our chances at trial. He gave us the news we wanted to hear. He felt we had a decent chance of winning, which is as good as you'll ever get from a libel lawyer. We had cleared another hurdle, but it felt like there was still a long and lonely way to go.

Then came Michael Bromell's intervention.

In our short meeting in my office, Bromell was frank about his past crimes and misdemeanours. He was an armed robber. If the police lifted him for a job he'd done, then OK: "I'll do my time." But he had served five years for wounding because the police had tampered with the evidence. He was adamant that he was innocent, he wanted justice, and he was taking his case to appeal. He was aware that our libel case involved the same officers he claimed had fitted him up and he told me he'd instructed his lawyers to do anything they could to help us. This was, as we journalists like to say, a bombshell.

There wasn't much more to discuss, so I thanked him, we shook hands and he turned to leave. On his way to the door, he stopped and asked if I could give him a tenner for a taxi home. The only thing in my mind at this point was to get on the phone to Nick Alway ASAP to tell him about Bromell's sensational offer of cooperation, so his request for cash caught me off guard. I gathered my thoughts and told him that, in view of what we had just agreed, it was probably best if no money changed hands. Fair enough, he said. At that moment, Coventry's Most Notorious cut a pathetic figure. And I breathed a sigh of relief that I wouldn't have to justify an expense claim that read: Taxi for armed robber, £10.

We had to wait a few months for Bromell's appeal to be heard but when it finally came to court, things moved quickly. Thanks to his offer of help, our legal team was in the Court of Appeal when he won his case, after Lord Taylor indicated there was a "very real possibility" the officers removed notes that could have proved Bromell's innocence.

The following month, our case came to the Court of Appeal, again in front of Lord Taylor. In an unprecedented ruling, he ordered that documents being held by the Police Complaints Authority should be disclosed to us, to help us defend the libel action brought by the two officers. The PCA had resisted our attempts to gain access to the documents because, they argued, disclosing them to a newspaper could deter people from coming forward in future to assist in their investigations.

Lord Taylor told the court: "If, as both [*Coventry Newspapers Ltd*] and the wider public now have every reason to suspect, these documents appear to point clearly towards corruption on the part of named officers, it is surely not to be tolerated that those same officers should continue to mulct the press in damages whilst the courts disable their adversaries from an effective defence by withholding the documents from them." And with those comments from the judge, the libel case against us evaporated.

Fighting libel actions is an expensive, emotionally draining business. Even when they know they have a strong case, publishers decide more often than not to settle, rather than risk the crippling cost of taking the action to court.

So this was a rare and hard-won victory for Her Majesty's Press. With a little help from an armed robber.

Chapter Eleven

A City Convulsed by Scandal

The unmasking of "celebrity" priest Christopher Clonan as a serial paedophile began when a 22-year-old drug addict turned up at the *Coventry Evening Telegraph* reception desk, asking to speak to a reporter. A few minutes later, sitting in a small, private office, he told crime reporter Sue Lary his story.

He came from a devout Catholic family and, to the delight of his parents, had been an altar boy at their local church. But as a teenager his life had descended rapidly into drug taking and violent behaviour, culminating in a jail sentence. He was in no doubt what had triggered his downward spiral. It was the result, he said, of the sexual abuse he endured at the hands of Father Clonan during a junior football trip to Ireland.

Now, 11 years later, he wanted the story of his ordeal to be told. His testimony triggered a story that not only scandalised the city of Coventry but would have ramifications across the globe. It prompted similar allegations of abuse against priests in numerous countries, sending shockwaves through the Catholic Church for years to come.

Clonan was a larger-than-life character, often to be seen driving his open-topped car around the Coundon area of Coventry or enjoying a drink and a cigar. Before becoming an assistant parish priest, he had run a small building firm and was much loved by the city's large Catholic community for rebuilding the Christ the King Club. Along the way, he picked up the nickname Father Fix-it.

The *Evening Telegraph* had documented his work at Christ the King, and one of the many pictures in our files showed him beaming at the camera as he worked on the club's new roof. Of course, any allegations of child sex abuse against a priest are incredibly serious but Clonan's special standing among the city's Catholics – many of whom were also loyal *Telegraph* readers – made this story potentially incendiary. We knew we had to tread with extreme care.

The young man told us he had made a complaint to the police, but when crime reporter Lary tried to have an off-the-record discussion for background purposes, her normally helpful police contacts would confirm only the barest facts. We needed further corroboration before we could run a story, so on Page 2 of the next day's edition, we went on a fishing expedition. We published an article, intentionally short on specific detail, reporting that a 22-year-old man had lodged a formal complaint to police that a West Midlands priest had sexually abused him during a trip to Ireland.

By the end of the same day, six more young men had contacted us, saying they had suffered similar abuse. All of them had been altar boys at Christ the King Church or had visited the youth club attached to it. And all of them named Clonan as their abuser. They had been between eight and 17 years old at the time. We advised them to report their allegations to the police.

A day or two later, when we contacted the police to confirm they had received further complaints, they continued to play it ultra-cautiously. They, too, knew the stakes were unusually high. We contacted senior members of the Catholic Church in the West Midlands, with whom the *Telegraph* had a strong relationship going back many years. They refused to say anything, on or off the record. The police then confirmed they had interviewed Clonan but at this stage he had not been charged.

News editor Peter Mitchell was pushing hard for us to publish the story but I had some reservations. On one hand, police inquiries were at an early stage and might not result in charges, so if we published we could stand accused of recklessly trashing a priest's reputation – and at the same time do irreparable damage to our own. On the other hand, we had the testimony of seven men who had described, independently and in detail, how, when, where and by whom they had been abused. Their testimony was so specific and similar they could not possibly be making it up. We ran the story past our lawyers, who said it was legally sound, and I decided to splash on it.

An hour or so later, with our print deadline approaching, I walked over to chief sub Charles Barker to see how Page One was coming along. He showed me a proof with the headline, in huge type, **PRIEST IN CHILD SEX PROBE** – accompanied by a full-length picture of Clonan in his vestments, in church. It was very stark and very bold. There was no going back.

Minutes later, after the presses had begun to roll and copies of the paper were shared out among the newsroom staff, there was an excited, nervous buzz in the air. News editor Mitchell walked towards me brandishing his copy of the paper and said: "Brave decision, boss." At that moment, it really was not what I needed to hear.

It wasn't long before the phones began to ring. We were inundated with calls from readers, some of them furious, some in tears, and all of them outraged that we had run the story. Many made the point that Clonan had not been charged with anything.

I asked the switchboard to direct all calls to assistant editor Alan Kirby, who was briefed to explain to callers that we stood by the story and that we had information, which could not yet be published for legal reasons, that made us confident that running the story was the right decision. Kirby spent the next several days with the phone jammed to his ear.

Amid the ensuing furore, Clonan disappeared from the city. With the Catholic authorities remaining silent and with little to go on from the police, we decided to send one of our most experienced journalists, Steve Chilton, to Clonan's home village in County Meath, Ireland, to talk to the locals. Within moments of his arrival at the village pub, he was told in the bluntest of terms to get out and head back to England. Sensibly, he beat a retreat.

Back in Coventry, Chilton kept digging and eventually learned that Clonan had fled to Ireland and checked himself into a hospital that specialised in psychiatric counselling and the treatment of alcoholism. Meanwhile, the police inquiry into the allegations against him stalled because, they said, there was insufficient evidence.

Over the next 12 years, the story takes several bizarre twists. After hospital treatment in Ireland, Clonan flies to Sydney. Police in Britain and Australia try to follow him but by the time their investigations begin the trail has gone cold. It is suspected that he moved to Melbourne, where his mother and brother Andrew were living.

Then, in 1998 – six years after he had been revealed as a paedophile and five years after I had left Coventry – it was reported that Clonan had died suddenly, of a brain haemorrhage. His brother said he was found in his apartment in the former gold-rush town of Kangaroo Flat, 90 miles north of Melbourne. He had been living a double life as 'Christy Oliver' (a combination of his given names Christopher Oliver) and, according to his brother, had been drinking three bottles of whiskey a day.

The funeral took place a few days later and the body was cremated – unusual for a Catholic priest, where burial is the norm. His family said they had chosen cremation because they were "financially challenged". The family sent a copy of the death certificate and photographs of Clonan lying in his coffin to the UK. But this failed to lay the story to rest – a legal source close to the case remarking it was the only time he had seen a corpse laughing. Initially, West Midlands police weren't buying it either. They suspected the shamed priest had faked his death to escape extradition to Britain.

In January 2004, the Catholic Church finally accepted responsibility for the damage Clonan had caused to many young lives and paid record out-of-court compensation to one of his victims. But if the Church hoped that would draw a line under this appalling episode, they were mistaken. More cases were brought to court on behalf of his victims, and they told a story of regular, long-term abuse leading, in some instances, to severe mental health problems.

Three months later, it was reported that Clonan had been spotted in the King's Heath area of Birmingham. A source with close links to the Catholic church said several priests had seen him at a church in the city, and that he was travelling under a new identity and posing as a teacher. However, the police finally said they were satisfied he had died in 1998, after taking DNA evidence from the crematorium in Australia.

The Clonan case was the catalyst for numerous allegations of abuse involving Catholic priests across the Western world. After one of the court hearings brought by one of the "celebrity" priest's victims, Peter Jennings, a spokesman for the Archdiocese of Birmingham, said the damage caused was "deep and lasting", adding that Clonan would "have to answer for his behaviour before the throne of God."

Chapter Twelve

Lonely Are the Brave

'Brave decision, boss." News editor Peter Mitchell's words after we had published one of the most explosive stories in the 100-year history of the *Coventry Evening Telegraph*, brought home to me how lonely life as an editor can be.

Decisions on controversial content are usually taken only after considerable discussion and debate by a group of senior newsroom executives. Sometimes, when the circumstances are particularly tricky, editors will seek the wise counsel of trusted colleagues elsewhere in the industry. But once the decision to publish is taken, it is the editor alone who must own the consequences. Terry Quinn put in neatly. "The great thing about being an editor," he said, "is that it's your train set and you get to play with it every day. But when it crashes, it's you that has to clean up the mess."

As an editor, your work is on show every day, and it's never perfect. You are there to be shot at, and the shots fly in from many directions. From readers, from your managing director, from your staff, from irate advertisers, from anyone with an axe to grind, and – these days – from any anonymous online troll who takes against you. Praise is generally slow to come and is hard-won. You're only as good as your last cock-up, and they tend to be quite public.

To be absolutely clear about it, editing is a wonderful job and was the greatest privilege of my career; I consider myself enormously lucky to have occupied the editor's chair at two of the UK's leading regional titles. But I also had my share of lonely moments. Like the day I was served with a £1 million libel writ, for example.

I was in my office at the *Evening Chronicle*, Newcastle, when a member of the reception staff rang and told me I must come down to the foyer straight away; a visitor had something that had to be handed to me in person. Waiting on the ground floor was a polite young man from a local law practice who gave me an envelope on behalf of a heavyweight London firm who specialised in high-profile defamation cases. I signed to acknowledge receipt of the writ and the young man vamoosed.

Back in my office, I opened the envelope and began to read. The London lawyers were acting on behalf of a businesswoman who had featured in a recent story on the front page of the *Chronicle*. (I'm taking care to keep this vague, in order to avoid another legal letter). They reckoned our story was highly libellous and they intended to sue the company for £1 million, and me personally for a further million.

In one way, this was laughable: thanks to my disastrous property purchase in Northampton, if Jo and I had sold everything we owned, we would have struggled to raise a few thousand pounds. In another way, it was highly unusual: normally, the newspaper or the publishing company would be cited as the defendant in a libel case, and not the editor*. A tricky phone call with our company secretary ensued. My starting position was: "Of course, you'll be indemnifying me against any personal financial risk … won't you?" To which he gave an equivocal and therefore far-from-reassuring reply.

We spoke to our lawyers, who were bullish at first but as the weeks rolled by their enthusiasm began to cool. After some deliberation, they reckoned that if the case went to court, we had a 60-70 per cent chance of winning. As editors know only too well, the stratospheric cost of court proceedings means that 60-70 per cent in your favour represents too much of a risk to the business. So we made the commercially-prudent decision and agreed to settle. It cost the company a small-five-figure sum, and it cost me a few nights of lost sleep and the indignity of publishing an apology for a story which I still believe was 100 per cent correct and justified.

Another lonely moment at the *Chronicle* came courtesy of our sister title, *The Journal*. I had been in Newcastle around six months and was meeting resistance from some members of staff who didn't like the editorial changes I had been brought in to make. The situation worsened when I heard on the grapevine that my ultimate bosses in London were starting to question some of my editorial content decisions. Alone in my office in the early evening, after all of my staff had left, I was preparing for a series of disciplinary meetings the next day. It was a hard grind and tomorrow was going to be gruelling for all concerned.

*Over the past 20 years or so, times have changed, and suing the editor is now something of a blood sport.

As I was reading the HR documents, there was a burst of raucous laughter in the newsroom followed by the sound of champagne corks popping. I stuck my head round the door to see *Journal* editor Neil Fowler and his team celebrating the latest in a truckload of awards for his title's highly successful conversion to tabloid format. As my fellow editor rode the crest of a wave, I was down in the dumps and feeling very alone. Over the next few months, I cheered myself up by poaching three of his best staff.

But none of my darker moments compares to the day one of my Scottish colleagues was pinned against the newsroom wall by an angry, drink-fuelled gangster, who had taken umbrage at the paper's coverage of his brother's murder in a drugs turf war.

Following an afternoon in the pub, the drug baron stormed into the paper's reception area, vaulted over the counter and ran upstairs to the editorial department, demanding to know "which one of you is the f****** editor?" Perhaps it was the look of terror on his face or maybe one of his staff helpfully pointed the finger, but within seconds the editor was being held by the throat and told in precise detail how his paper would cover the murdered brother's funeral in the following week's edition. The uninvited guest editor's instructions were carried out to the letter, which, in the circumstances, was probably a very wise decision.

* * * *

Editors come in a variety of shapes and sizes, but until the late Eighties they came almost exclusively in the shape of a man. In the majority of cases they were intimidating, and none more so than Ted Dickinson, Northern editor of the *Daily Express*.

Over the winter of 1978-79, as a young sub at *The Star*, in Sheffield, I was moonlighting on the *Express*'s Manchester features desk, to earn a little pin money and in the hope of landing a full-time job. The *Daily Star* had just been launched and the newsroom and composing room had been split down the middle – one half for *Express*, the other for the upstart *Star*. The *Express* staff had also been split across the two titles, which meant a large number of casual sub-editors was required in order to get the papers out.

For young subs like me, this was the California Gold Rush. Every day, cars full of hopefuls would head for Manchester from all parts of the North. In my case, it meant driving my hopelessly unreliable Mini over the Woodhead Pass, often in awful weather, and praying I'd make it back in one piece.

I'd been doing casual shifts for several months when features editor Ron Baker pulled me to one side to say he'd lined up a job interview. Editor Dickinson would see me before the start of my shift the following week. Ron told me not to worry, he was recommending me and it would all be fine, just a matter of going through the formalities. So I turned up outside the editor's office for my interview feeling pretty confident.

At 6ft 3in, broad-shouldered and wearing a perpetual frown, Dickinson cut an imposing figure. He motioned me to sit as he eased himself into his chair, plonked his sizeable, brown-brogued feet on his desk and picked up my letter of application. After what felt like an eternity, he broke the silence. "So, you're 24. You've done a few shifts. What makes you think I should give you a job at the *Daily Express*?"

As opening questions go, this was quite a tester. I was in there a few minutes but, frankly, I can't remember anything else about the interview. I emerged from his office to start my shift, feeling like a schoolboy who had been given six of the best by the headmaster. A week later, I received a letter offering me the job.

If Dickinson's interviewing style wasn't straight out of the personnel department handbook, it was topped a few years later when I met Dennis Hackett, then editor of the short-lived *Today* newspaper and a man with a distinguished career in national newspapers and magazines under his belt. His chief sub-editor, John Honeywell, a friend from our *Express* days, told me *Today* was looking for subs and he wondered if I was interested. I was, and when I turned up for my interview appointment at lunchtime on March 17, John sat me down in a waiting room and told me the editor would be back in a few minutes.

After an hour or so, there was still no sign of Mr Hackett. John apologised for the delay, sorted out a cup of tea for me and moved me into the editor's office. Another hour passed. John got me more tea and said he was sure the boss would be back shortly. Hackett finally turned up, after what had obviously been a long and convivial lunch. He looked somewhat put out to see a stranger lurking in his office – it was clear he had completely forgotten about our meeting. Whatever his plans for the rest of the afternoon, I got the impression it didn't involve conducting a job interview.

There was no hint of an apology but, by way of explanation, Hackett said he'd been out to celebrate St Patrick's Day. "Oh,' I said, trying to build a rapport with my potential employer, "do you have some Irish blood?" "No," he said. The interview lasted a painful 20 minutes, with him struggling to ask a sensible question and me thinking there's no way on Earth I'm coming to work here. As I left, he told me he'd be in touch. I never heard from him again.

But both Dickinson and Hackett paled in comparison to one of Dickinson's predecessors as *Express* Northern editor, a certain 'Strangler'* Lewis. Assistant features editor Bob Ward told me a tale that had gone down in *Express* folklore of a young reporter who came over from Ireland for a job interview. His appointment was scheduled for mid-afternoon but bad weather delayed his ferry crossing, and he arrived at the *Express* building wet, bedraggled and several hours late.

Apparently, it was customary during Mr Lewis's tenure that after the first edition had been put to bed, the whole backbench team would repair to the editor's office for a reviving dram. This could turn into quite a session, often involving a full-throated sing-song.

When the interviewee finally made it to the *Express* newsroom and asked where he might find the editor, the hard-pressed chief sub – up to his neck in the second edition – pointed him in the direction of the singing. Timidly, the reporter knocked at the door. One of the backbenchers ushered him in, bringing the singing to an abrupt stop.

Strangler: "Who the f*** are you?"

Reporter: "I'm here for a job interview. I'm terribly sorry I'm late but the ferry..."

Strangler: "Can you sing?"

Reporter: "Er yes, a wee bit."

Strangler (noting the interviewee's accent): "Right, stand on that chair and give us two choruses of Danny Boy."

> **I have been unable to establish whether 'Strangler' was his given name or a nickname he picked up along the way. I like the idea of his mother summoning him as a young boy with: 'Strangler, love, your tea's ready!'*

Apparently, the young Irishman had the voice of an angel and was appointed to a staff reporting role on the strength of his performance.

* * * *

The *Express* newsroom was buzzing with speculation after Ted Dickinson announced he had been promoted and would soon be heading to London as deputy editor. We were all itching to know who the new Northern editor would be and, as is the way with journalists, a plethora of runners and riders was suggested – some plausible, some left-field, some entertainingly outlandish. A few days later, it was announced that the baton would pass to Tony Fowler. He was a new name to me but had worked in Manchester previously and was well known to the older hands.

Stories from Tony's earlier stint in Manchester began circulating, which illustrated the intense way in which he approached the job. Two tales stood out. In the early Seventies, when Tony had done his previous stint in Manchester, the *Express* was a broadsheet and was still using the hot metal production process. Unlike modern desktop publishing, where everything is fitted neatly on to the page at the sub-editing stage, hot metal was inherently imprecise, and stories often had to be shoe-horned into the page in the composing room. It was standard practice for a number of news-in-brief paragraphs (known by sub-editors as NIBs) to be sent to the composing room as standbys, to be slotted into the page if a story fell short and a hole needed to be filled.

In his days as the sub-editor responsible for Page One, Tony's instruction to the stone sub was to fit at least eight NIBs on to the front page, to give it a busy, newsy feel. But some NIBs were more important than others, so to make sure the stone sub chose correctly, the essential ones would be marked "MUST NIB". One night, while checking a proof of the front page, he began to boil with rage when he saw that some of his MUST NIBS hadn't made it. He grabbed the phone to harangue the stone sub:

TF: "I THOUGHT I TOLD YOU TO USE THE MUST NIBS FIRST."

Stone sub: "Yes Tony, you did. But there's only space for eight and you sent 15 of them."

TF (after a short silence): 'RIGHT! I'M STARTING A NEW SYSTEM! FROM NOW ON, THERE ARE NIBS, THERE ARE MUST NIBS AND THERE ARE MUST MUST NIBS!'

On another memorable night, Tony received a call from a composing room manager, telling him cuts were needed urgently on the Page One splash, in order to get the edition away by deadline. OK, says Tony, I'll send someone, and he dispatches a sub-editor. Dashing down to the composing room, the sub jumps down the last few stairs, lands awkwardly and breaks his ankle. Writhing in pain, he is found by a member of the composing room staff, who calls an ambulance. A few minutes later, Tony's phone rings again.

Manager: "The edition's late and we're still waiting for cuts on Page One. When are you going to get somebody down here?"

TF: "I sent Pete quarter of an hour ago."

Manager: "Pete's in Ancoats Hospital with a broken ankle."

TF (with his head in his hands): "Why does it always happen to me?"

After a few months of his editorship, it was obvious that Tony was an extremely accomplished journalist, who demanded the highest standards from his staff. But a volcanic eruption was never far from the surface, which tended to suppress creativity – the subs quickly realising that keeping your head down was a better option than having it bitten off.

* * * *

One of the big characters among my contemporaries as a regional editor was Ranald Allan. An ebullient Aberdonian, he had made his name as editor of the *Reading Evening Post* and was rewarded with a promotion to a bigger title within Thomson Newspapers, the *Teesside Evening Gazette*. Ranald was famed for his love of Indian food, which bordered on an addiction. The frequency of his lunchtime visits to the curry house across the road from the *Gazette* office prompted the owner to name him their Most Loyal Customer and present him with a personalised discount card.

Ranald became known for a tendency to "rest his eyes" during afternoon management meetings. Some put this down to his lunchtime diet but the cause was later diagnosed as sleep apnoea, a condition which causes your breathing to stop and start while sleeping, disturbing your rest and leaving you tired during the day.

One year, at the opening of the Society of Editors' annual conference, Ranald, Journal editor Neil Fowler and I sat alongside each other to hear the President's opening address. We had shared a long train journey from the North East to the South Coast and had lunched well. In the late afternoon, as the President took to the stage and the house lights were dimmed, Fowler and I swapped pieces of paper with our guess as to how many minutes it would be before Ranald was in the Land of Nod. Both of us overestimated it grossly.

These days, with revenues under pressure and budgets constrained, industry conferences aren't quite what they used to be. In the good times, I had the opportunity to visit a number of exotic locations, from World Editors' Forums in Gothenburg, Hong Kong and Cape Town to a Society of Editors seminar in Grimsby. While the Society's venues were not always the most glamorous, the annual conference was always a highlight, where editors, media academics and sponsors would come together for a couple of days of discussion and social high jinks.

Relationships between working editors and academics are not always entirely cordial. Some academics are convinced they know more about journalism than the practitioners, while some editors are firmly of the view that "Those who can, do. Those who can't, teach". At an annual conference in Glasgow, this fractious relationship came to the surface during a debate on training.

After a presentation by Derek Tucker, then editor of the *Press & Journal*, in Aberdeen, an academic known for his dim view of all newsroom managers made some provocative remarks about the level of educational attainment among regional editors. In his view, expressed at inordinate length, appointing people of a higher academic calibre to the editor's chair was the key to solving the industry's woes. Taking the insult personally, Tucker shot back: "I'll have you know that I have a first-class honours degree in Classics from Oxford." This silenced the academic and ended the debate.

In the bar afterwards, I told Tucker, who I'd known for some years, that I wasn't aware he had an Oxford degree. "I don't," he said, "but it shut that f***** up, didn't it?"

There's a camaraderie among editors, probably because we all feel we've been asked to steer the same leaky bathtub around Cape Horn in the teeth of a gale. At the same time, there's a strong element of professional rivalry. In Nineties Newcastle, home to two daily titles and a Sunday, each with its own editor and separate editorial staffs, the competitive edge was especially keen.

The three titles were aimed at different markets – *The Journal* at the region's business community and the residents of rural Northumberland, the *Chronicle* at Tyneside families and the *Sunday Sun* at blue-collar readers across the wider North – but the three reporting teams fought tooth-and-nail to win the news battle. It made for good fun and good papers.

One of the biggest stories in my time as editor of the *Chronicle* was the murder of notorious Tyneside hard man Viv Graham, gunned down in the street on New Year's Eve. From my point of view, the killer's timing couldn't have been worse.

Graham, a former amateur boxer, made his money by organising club doormen across Tyneside, while running an extortion racket on the side. He had a fearsome reputation for violence and had served time in jail for a ferocious assault on a rival doorman. The victim refused to give evidence but the brutal beating had been captured on CCTV. After his release, Graham locked horns with a number of drug gangs, which led to several attempts on his life.

On New Year's Eve 1993, as he walked along Wallsend High Street with a copy of the *Evening Chronicle* tucked under his arm, he was shot three times by a drive-by assassin in a Ford Escort. Graham, who often said he wouldn't see 40, died in North Tyneside General Hospital four hours later. He was 34.

What made the timing so bad for the *Chronicle* was that the shooting happened a few hours after our New Year's Eve edition had been printed. With no web site in those days, we had no means of covering the story until after the Bank Holiday weekend. That was three days away, and by then the local radio and TV stations, as well as our sister newspapers had swarmed all over this shocking murder.

On the morning of January 4, I arrived at the office to find we had no new angles for that day's edition. But if ever there was a '*Chronicle* story', this was it. I told the news desk to throw all their resources at finding new lines on the killing. We had no pictures to support the story, so illustrator Geoff Laws was tasked with creating an artist's impression of the moment Graham was shot. Meanwhile, crime reporter Brenda Hickman, just back from holiday, started working her police contacts.

The whole team responded brilliantly. We secured an exclusive interview with Graham's girlfriend, followed a day or two later by an interview with another woman who, unknown to the girlfriend, was in a long-term relationship with Graham and had children by him.

Each story we broke led to another. The police wanted to work with us, because the publicity could help them in the murder inquiry, and Graham's family were keen to talk. From a cold, stuttering start, the *Chronicle* snatched ownership of the story from the rest of the North East media – and the exclusives kept on coming.

Coverage of Graham's murder and his luridly-colourful life led our front page for 14 consecutive editions. A few readers rang in to complain, telling us they had had their fill of Graham, and one or two accused us of glorifying him. But the newspaper sales graph doesn't lie; it showed that Tyneside could not get enough of this story, and we were eager to oblige. Journalistically, it was one of my team's finest moments, and I could not have been more proud of them.

But despite more than 1,000 police interviews, the offer of a £100,000 reward by his family and blanket coverage in the media, the murder of Viv Graham remains unsolved.

* * * *

Thomson Newspapers editorial director Stuart Garner would sometimes express the slightly controversial view that the editor "doesn't need to be the best journalist in the room". His point was that there were plenty of experienced, highly competent people in the newsroom who were more than capable of putting together a good paper and, in his opinion, editors should step back from the day-to-day operation, to take a more strategic view. Look to the future, plan the title's development, play a bigger role from the wider business perspective.

My old colleague Ranald Allan had a neat take on this. "My deputy's job," he said, "is to make sure the paper comes out today. My job is to make sure it comes out in six months' time." But hands-on journalism is a powerful drug and, despite what the editorial director said, some editors of my generation had no intention of giving up their daily fix in favour of writing a 12-month brand development plan.

My experience was that getting stuck in and demonstrating your ability as a sharp-end journalist every now and then was a powerful way for an editor to earn credibility with your staff. At the same time, it's important not to let the balance tip over into self-indulgence, spending too much time doing what you enjoy the most and leaving the bigger picture unattended.

In the final analysis, editors are judged on how good they are at steering the ship, not stoking the boiler. It has to be said that today's editors don't have the luxury of choosing between being hands-on and hands-off; the economics of modern publishing demand that they do both.

I was fortunate to edit two of the UK's leading regional dailies during times of plenty. To quote a commercial colleague: "In those days, the money was flying in through the windows." Despite a continuous, gentle decline since the end of World War Two, sales of newspapers remained extremely strong through the Eighties and Nineties. When I moved to Newcastle in 1993, the *Chronicle* was selling around 125,000 copies, six nights a week, in a conurbation of approximately 350,000 people. At the time, local radio reached just two or three per cent of the local population. In towns and cities across the UK, the story was the same – for news, sport and local advertising, the evening paper was the only game in town.

Soon after I moved to Newcastle, managing director Tony Hill gave me the task of setting up "The 125 Club" – a group of regional editors whose titles were selling 125,000 copies a night or more. Around seven papers qualified for membership, including the *Chronicle*, the *Yorkshire Evening Post*, the *Manchester Evening News* and the *Wolverhampton Express & Star**. Tony's idea was that we would exchange proven editorial and promotional ideas, to help all of us support our sales.

> **According to Audit Bureau of Circulations figures, sales of the Express & Star (for many years Britain's top-selling regional title) fell from 217,000 a night in 1994 to just over 20,000 in 2020. Virtually every other title in the UK has suffered a similar percentage decline.*

After a couple of months, Tony asked if I'd made any progress with the 125 Club. I told him I'd been a bit tied up, getting to know the staff, introducing content improvements, dealing with the most pressing newsroom issues, meeting key players in the city. "OK," he said. "but if you leave it much longer, we'll have to rename it the f****** 120 Club."

On the back of newspaper sales that remained relatively strong, advertising revenue powered ahead and profits continued to grow. This meant the resources at an editor's disposal were still considerable, even though it may not have felt like it at the time. When I took the editor's chair in Coventry in 1991, managing director Ernest Petrie told me "economies" were required. After an arm-wrestle (which I was never going to win), we agreed I would lose eight members of my team. This reduced the editorial staff from 92 to 84 – riches that regional editors would find unimaginable today.

I had always loved the immediacy of evening papers, and the idea of giving readers the freshest on-the-day news from their city. But evening titles enjoyed several other unique selling points, far removed from the world of breaking news. For example, billboards promoting "Tomorrow's racecards tonight" were a common sight outside newsagents. Evening titles had unique access to the most up-to-date information on runners and riders for the following day's meetings, which meant punters could settle down in the evening with their local paper and make their selections from the comfort of their armchair.

The reader value of publishing the latest racecard was often lost on those editors with no interest in horseracing, who would see it as an inordinate amount of space given over to a minority interest. In the mid-Eighties, a regional editor in the South West decided to scrap the racecards, only to be forced to reinstate them within a week following a fusillade of complaints from racing-mad readers.

The chastened editor commissioned his cartoonist to draw a sketch of him hiding in a trench, wearing a tin helmet and waving a white flag, which he ran on Page One, alongside the announcement that the racecards were being brought back forthwith. As ignominious climbdowns go, this one was executed with a touch of style.

But times have moved on. Today, the sophistication and depth of online form guides, available at any time of the reader's choosing, has removed the evening paper's unique advantage, prompting a number of editors to drop racecards entirely, without so much as a whimper from readers.

It wasn't just the racecards that were superseded by new, online equivalents. As late as the early Noughties, a major survey conducted for Trinity Mirror showed conclusively that three 'landmark' pieces of non-news content were still of primary importance to most regional newspaper readers – the family announcements (births, marriages and deaths) column, the readers' letters page and the nightly TV listings spread. All three were proven to drive sales of the newspaper.

But, over the course of 10 years, the tradition of readers placing 'hatches, matches and dispatches' advertisements in their local paper and penning letters to the editor have been largely killed off, principally by the march of social media. I can understand why anyone would baulk at paying hundreds of pounds for a four-line wedding announcement when you can tell your family and friends for free on Facebook.

And the daily TV guide, a staple ingredient of newspapers since the Sixties, has been rendered largely redundant by a combination of the electronic programme guide and viewers abandoning linear TV for on-demand services. How long will it be until the TV spread disappears from newspapers entirely?

The biggest change of all for evening newspaper editors was when their titles switched from on-the-day printing and distribution, to overnight. On-the-day production required a large fleet of vans and drivers to distribute the papers speedily across the circulation area, in a very narrow time window. Printing overnight – in effect, becoming a morning paper – meant copies could be distributed through the wholesale trade, used by the national morning papers.

Piggybacking the existing network in this way saved considerable cost – in the region of £1 million a year for a large evening title – which was impossible to ignore at a time when publishers were seeing advertising revenue migrate to the web at an alarming rate. Where else could we find a £1 million saving in a single hit? More cuts in editorial staffing, perhaps? Nevertheless, for some evening paper editors this was the bitterest pill of all to swallow. For a few, it marked the point where they walked away.

If the digital age has had a fundamental impact on newspaper content, the impact on journalists – from trainees through to the editor – has been even greater. Every journalist's job has become wider, deeper, more complex, more technology-focused and more multi-faceted. Whatever branch of the media you work in, doing much more, with much less resource, is the name of the game – and that applies most acutely in those businesses whose heritage is the printed newspaper.

Print remains an important element, not least because it still drives much of the revenue, but digital is where the audience (and the future) is, so understanding web sites, apps, video, social media, digital analytics and audience engagement is absolutely essential. It's a far cry from the days when the editor's main tasks were to decide what went on Page One and having the occasional bust-up with the advertising director.

Prior to the digital revolution, newspaper companies – like most businesses – were strongly hierarchical. Staff were expected to defer to the boss, who was always right. Even when he wasn't. Today, the wide range of technical skills required of journalists and the plethora of platforms we work on call for a different approach to newsroom leadership. Editors have had to adjust to the fact that they may no longer be the most knowledgeable journalist in the room, and that their staff – often the youngest, least-experienced ones – have far superior digital skills and know-how.

So if you're an editor who is not a digital native, the job now is less about rolling up your sleeves and leading from the front, and more about providing wise counsel and leading from the back. A bit less Han Solo and a bit more Yoda, you might say. I wonder what Strangler Lewis would have made of it?

Chapter Thirteen

Beneath the Waterline

O nly once have I been in a position to utter the immortal line: 'Hold the front page!'* We were a couple of minutes away from putting the first edition of the *Chronicle* to bed when my PA shouted across the newsroom: "Michael Heseltine is on the phone for you." Heseltine, the deputy Prime Minister, was calling with the news that a deal had been struck with German electronics giant Siemens to build a £1.1 billion microprocessor factory on North Tyneside, bringing with it 2,000 desperately-needed jobs.

The old smoothie told me he was aware of our deadlines and he was sure that, as the leading paper in the region, we'd want to be first with the news. I asked him for a quote for our article, which he provided off the cuff, with the polish you'd expect. Then I scooted over to the Page One sub and dictated the new splash to him, off the top of my head. Within minutes, the rejigged front page was away.

This sticks in my mind because it was obviously a big story for the region, and it's not every day the deputy Prime Minister rings you. It was also one of the relatively few days, in my time as an editor, that I committed a serious act of hands-on journalism.

A regional editor's life is like an iceberg – there's the bit the world can see (the newspaper) but there's a whole lot more going on beneath the waterline. I'd estimate that 20 per cent of my time as editor – at most – was focused on sharp-end journalism, and even that was a largely vicarious thrill, as mostly it involved chairing the morning and afternoon news conferences, where the news, features and sports editors present their proposed lists of content. In effect, they are "selling" to the editor decisions they have already made. Of course, the editor has the final say but mostly it's a case of marking someone else's homework.

I didn't actually say it, as I'd have sounded a right prat.

The other 80 per cent of my time was filled with a million and one other things. There were the usual business-related activities – management meetings, dealing with legal issues, staffing matters, replying to complaints, glad-handing advertisers, representing the paper at outside events. Then there were the unexpected bits: a major advertiser threatening to pull their spend because they didn't like a story you'd published or a run-in with the local football club.

Generally speaking, football clubs have a love-hate relationship with their local paper. When a new regime takes over a club, it's all hearts and flowers, but the love-in can descend quickly into a whole heap of bitterness and recrimination, often with a side order of a reporting ban. The breakdown is usually triggered by a predictable chain of events – a poor run of results, the spectre of relegation, the fans getting restless, the manager coming under pressure and reacting by lashing out. He knows that criticising the fans directly is a short cut to the Job Centre, so instead he directs his fury at the "voice of the fans" – the local paper.

My first close encounter with an angry manager was when *Telegraph & Argus* editor Mike Glover and I were invited by Bradford City chairman Jack Tordoff to hold "clear the air" talks with him and manager Terry Yorath. Not for the first time, the club was unhappy with the way the *T&A* had been reporting on events at Valley Parade. The previous chairman, millionaire businessman Stafford Heginbotham, had launched a libel action against the paper, although it never came to court.

From the moment we entered the chairman's office, it was obvious Yorath was boiling with anger. The introductions were barely over when he launched into a tirade about our coverage, lasting several minutes. It was quite an outpouring but eventually the fire burnt itself out. I could sense that Glover was shaken (as I was) but he responded calmly, explaining the role of the local paper as the fans' mouthpiece, and standing by our coverage, which he believed had been fair and accurate. And that was just about it. Yorath had little else to say and a short, curious meeting was over.

Back at the office, as we reflected on the meeting, it struck me that – institutionally – football clubs were not dissimilar to the Army, with the manager in the role of sergeant major. Here was a man with 20 years' experience in his field, who as a player had been trained to take instructions and who, now he was in charge, expected his instructions to be followed

114

without question. But, faced with an outsider who was prepared to stand his ground, he wasn't sure how to react.

Today, the working relationship between clubs and local reporters is more distant, at Premier League level at least. Clubs don't see as much value in working with the occasionally-troublesome local press. Some papers are still given exclusive time with the manager but the days when the football reporter travelled to away matches on the team bus are long gone. And the enormous injection of money into the top end of the game, much of which finds its way into the players' bank accounts, has fundamentally changed the coach-player relationship too. Today's multi-millionaire players (and their agents) don't take orders meekly from anyone.

* * * *

The most salutary lesson I learned as an editor had its beginnings on a quiet Monday morning in Coventry. There wasn't much news about, and we were struggling to find a story strong enough to lead the front page. News editor Peter Mitchell geed up his reporters, urging them to ring their contacts to try to unearth a decent tale. As we approached our first edition deadline, we still didn't have anything, so we decided to promote a story that had originally been placed on Page 3, about a teenager who had fallen to his death from the city's ring road after a night out.

The accident had been covered extensively over the weekend by local TV and radio. We didn't have a new angle to take the story forward, so we didn't see it as a candidate for the front page. But in the absence of a strong, newer story, we decided to lead on the death, and to "beef it up" by injecting a few punchy adjectives. The night out became "a binge", his death the result of drink-fuelled recklessness. With the first edition put to bed, Mitchell set about finding a new splash for the main City edition.

In my morning post later that week there was a letter from the dead teenager's mother. It ran to a couple of pages. There was no anger. She asked simply if I could imagine what it was like to lose a child? Had I ever done anything stupid after a few drinks? Did I understand how painful it was to see her son described so coldly by her local paper?

She told me her 19-year-old son had come home for Christmas after his first term at university. Buzzing with excitement and with many stories to share, he had arranged a night on the town with his closest school friend. But, with one slip, their joyful reunion had ended in tragedy.

I spent most of the day thinking about the letter. There was no justification for the way we had treated the story, and the only decent response was to write back offering an unqualified apology for our insensitivity.

In an attempt to redress the balance, I asked if she would agree to be interviewed by our chief feature writer Barbara Argument, to tell the story of the son she knew. To my surprise, she said yes. Barbara, a mother of three and a wonderfully empathetic journalist, visited the family's home to do the interview and produced one of the most tender, touching articles I've ever read. It was accompanied by a selection of photos from the family album. As a piece of journalism, it was infinitely more powerful and compelling than our original, obtuse report.

After the interview was published, the young man's mother wrote to me again, thanking us for publishing the interview. I felt humbled that, in the depth of her grief, she had dealt with this terrible episode in such a gracious and forgiving way. I wouldn't make the same crass mistake again.

* * * *

Vendor contracts don't often set an editor's adrenaline pumping but an invitation to a top-secret meeting to discuss the axing of our biggest news supplier had me hooked.

The Press Association – Britain's national news agency – was founded in 1868 by a group of regional press proprietors who wanted a reliable London-based news service to supply their titles. Over the years, PA diversified its product range and its client base, which by the early Nineties spanned TV, radio and a variety of non-media clients. This made good business sense and provided the regional publishing groups, who still owned PA, with a tidy financial return. But in the early Nineties regional editors were less happy than their publisher bosses, feeling we were paying PA handsomely while our titles had slipped down their list of priorities.

Seven of us gathered for a working lunch, chaired jointly by two of the regional press's big hitters, Thomson Newspapers editorial director Stuart Garner and Midland Independent Newspapers CEO Chris Oakley. They stressed that our discussion was strictly confidential. Two of Oakley's editors

– Ian Dowell, of the *Birmingham Evening Mail*, and yours truly from the *Coventry Evening Telegraph* – were among the guests.

Before we had finished our starters, it was clear we all shared the view that PA wasn't giving us the attention or the value for money we expected. The conversation moved on to the idea of setting up a rival agency. This had a strong appeal, despite the huge effort and cost it would involve – an indication of the level of dissatisfaction around the table. The meeting broke up with an agreement that we should meet again in a few weeks to take the idea further.

The following Monday, all hell broke loose when UK Press Gazette, the newspaper industry's trade journal, splashed with an exclusive revealing that a "Gang of Seven" had held a clandestine meeting to plot the overthrow of PA. The report contained every salient detail – the venue, who was there, what had been discussed.

The source of the leak to Press Gazette remained a mystery but, by sheer coincidence, Thomson boss Garner struck an extremely keenly-priced, long-term deal with PA shortly afterwards. Our follow-up meeting never took place and the idea of launching a rival to PA was shelved.

Dissatisfaction persisted among the other publishing groups and a few years later Northcliffe Newspapers revived the idea of a rival agency but couldn't get the other big publishers on board. They decided to go it alone and set up UK News, run from their East Midlands heartland. But without the other publishers to augment their content offering, coverage was patchy and they struggled to match the PA service. After grinding it out for a handful of years, UK News was closed down.

* * * *

Five years later, and 200 miles further north, what looked like a rather more routine lunch meeting had surprisingly dramatic consequences. My deputy editor Alison Hastings and I met Northumbria Police chief constable John Stevens and his deputy David Mellish at a Newcastle restaurant for a routine catch-up. Towards the end of a pleasant meal, they fed us a tasty titbit of news concerning NCIS, the national crime agency, which reflected well on the Northumbria force. We ran it as an exclusive in the next day's edition.

As we were enjoying our lunch, the trial of Tyneside gang boss Paddy Conroy and three of his associates was drawing to a conclusion at Newcastle Crown Court. They were charged with the kidnap, torture and false imprisonment of rival gangster Billy Collier. Several gruesome acts of violence had been inflicted on Collier, including the removal of his teeth with a pair of pliers. If convicted, the four defendants were facing a lengthy prison term.

It had taken the authorities some time to bring Conroy to justice. He had been arrested and charged but, en route to a remand hearing, he and his co-accused escaped by overpowering their guards and jumping into a waiting getaway car. In the following months, rumours abounded regarding Conroy's whereabouts, the most colourful being that he was living in the West End of Newcastle, disguised as a woman. In fact, after a couple of months lying low in Gateshead he had slipped out of the country to Spain. Five months later, he was re-arrested at gunpoint as he sat in a car at Malaga Airport. After a year in custody in Spain, he was extradited to Britain.

The *Chronicle* had been reporting on the trial throughout, and it wasn't looking good for Conroy & Co. In a desperate last throw of the dice, their barristers claimed our NCIS story – which had no connection whatsoever with the Conroy case – showed some sort of collusion between Northumbria Police and the *Chronicle*, and called for a re-trial.

As he adjourned for lunch, the judge told *Chronicle* reporter Mick Smith he wanted the editor in court and ready to give evidence when proceedings re-started. Walking back to the office to relay the judge's message, Smith sensed he was being followed. As he neared the office, a man – presumably an associate of the defendants – closed in to whisper in his ear: "Do the right thing, Mick."

In the event, it was my deputy who attended court to face questioning by the defence lawyers. It quickly became obvious that our story had no bearing on the case and the request for a retrial was dismissed. The jury returned guilty verdicts and the judge sentenced Conroy to eleven and a half years behind bars.

And that was that. Until a policewoman turned up at my deputy's house to recommend she should have a panic alarm installed, at the force's expense, in case Conroy's associates sought revenge. A couple of nights later, in the early hours, I was shocked awake as bright lights and a huge noise enveloped our house. Half asleep and with my heart racing, I was sure Conroy's gang were on my doorstep, ready to wreak havoc. It turned out to be an Army helicopter on night-time manoeuvres.

* * * *

These days, anyone with a smartphone and a social media account is a publisher. But in the pre-digital Nineties, if you had a piece of news to share, you would very likely call your local paper.

When an angry warehouseman phoned the *Chronicle* with "something you should know about", the news editor wasn't too impressed at first. The caller explained that a kestrel had got into the furniture warehouse where he worked. It passed its time perched on the rafters, occasionally spreading its wings for a short flight. Unfortunately, Kes was also dropping numerous unwanted deposits on the thousands of pounds' worth of beds and sofas below. Mildly amusing, but not a contender for Page One at this stage. But there was more …

Unsure how he should deal with the situation, the warehouse manager rang the owner of the business. He knew precisely what to do, and turned up a little while later with an air gun. He took aim, fired, and missed. He tried again and this time scored a direct hit. Kes spiralled down, landing on the warehouse floor with a dull thud.

All the staff cheered their sharpshooter boss – except for our caller, who was incensed that the bird had been summarily despatched rather than the RSPCA being called, as he had suggested. The caller gave us some strong quotes, on an anonymous basis, and the RSPCA confirmed that shooting a bird of prey was illegal and they would be investigating. Now we had a decent story on our hands.

Our reporter called the business owner, who declined to comment. But within minutes, the *Chronicle*'s advertising director was knocking on my door. He would never try to influence editorial decisions, of course, but he just wanted to let me know that the deadeye director had just called him to say that if we ran the story, he would cancel his advertising contract. All £250,000 of it.

A sensible discussion ensued. We agreed that the advertising director would go back to the businessman to explain that suppressing news that we knew to be accurate was a non-starter; that if we didn't run the story, our source would almost certainly tip off other local media; and that he might want to think about giving us a quote explaining why he had to act quickly, to save any more of his expensive stock from being ruined, while also expressing regret for his actions. To our relief, he accepted our suggestions, we had our story and his advertising spend with the *Chronicle* remained intact.

* * * *

Maybe it's because the news industry is permanently focused on the here and now, but when it comes to taking care of our history, we haven't covered ourselves in glory. To take a by-no-means isolated example, the *Liverpool Echo*'s Beatles photographic files are surprisingly thin. The best material disappeared many years ago, when access was perhaps not monitored as strictly as it might have been, and some of those passing through the library were more aware of the pictures' commercial value than the owners.

It wasn't always thus. In the early-Seventies, the *Sheffield Star* had half a dozen full-time librarians, who policed their domain with the zeal of North Korean border guards. If a reporter wanted to remove a cuttings packet from the library, you had to sign it out and sign it back in again. And if the packet went missing, they came looking for you.

In some of the offices I worked in, the filing was done according to an established, conventional system. In others, it followed a logic that presumably made sense to the chief librarian but remained a mystery to everyone else.

Over the years, technology advanced and publishers began to store articles on microfiche. This saved space but, from a reporter's point of view, made the content harder to access, which was a pain in the neck if you needed a cutting in a hurry.

When digitisation came along, storage became cheap and access to newly-created material virtually instantaneous, from the journalist's desktop. This presented an opportunity to convert the archive – or even just the best and most-used parts of it – into an easy-to-use digital resource but proposals always hit the buffers on cost grounds. So our heritage, and the commercial value within it, remained in a hard-to-use smorgasbord of formats, the paper-based cuttings slowly and silently turning to dust.

As the industry came under increasing financial pressure, rather than treating the archive as the family silver, some publishers looked at the large amount of space taken up by racks of cuttings envelopes, photographic prints and bound newspaper volumes and saw a costly inconvenience.

As publishers downsized into smaller premises, some newsrooms lost their hard-copy archive entirely, and others have Swiss cheese-style holes. However, at the *Newcastle Chronicle* we did score one small success.

One afternoon, sub-editor Ray Marshall, who was responsible for compiling our nostalgia pages, popped his head round my office door, looking concerned. He told me he had been having a poke about in the company garage* and had spotted a skip, covered with a tarpaulin. He pulled it back to find hundreds of glass photographic plates from the Forties and Fifties that someone had decided (without consulting the editorial department) were surplus to requirements.

Ray picked a few off the top and saw they included action shots of legendary Newcastle United centre forward Jackie Milburn. A fragile, unique and irreplaceable record of one of Newcastle's greatest players, in action at St James's Park, dumped in a skip. The saving grace was that whoever had put the plates in there had done so with some care, as many were still intact.

Ray implored me to let him save the pictures. Over several weeks, alongside his day job, he sorted through them, retrieving the best material and having it converted into a more robust format. He then put together a supplement of Milburn in Action, which was a huge hit with Newcastle fans.

One of the news industry's biggest and best remaining photographic libraries is Reach plc's Watford photo archive, which houses several million images from the *Daily Mirror* and the company's regional titles. A selective and steady digitisation programme, taking care to house the archive in the correct atmospheric conditions, has helped to preserve this irreplaceable content for daily use and for posterity.

> *The garage was a dark, damp, dungeon-like tunnel, with one way in and out, which rendered it singularly ill-suited for vehicular access (not a great feature in a garage). It happened to contain a portion of the original, Grade One-listed, city wall, which made modernisation difficult.*

One of the greatest and most under-rated contributions regional newspapers make to local life is their community campaigning. Covering all manner of topics, from highlighting injustice to stimulating economic revival and raising cash for medical equipment, a well-targeted local newspaper campaign can produce tangible benefits that otherwise simply would not happen.

Most campaigns fall into Terry Quinn's "short, sharp and winnable" category, but occasionally an editor will decide it's important to go down with all guns blazing, even when you know the cause is lost. The *Chronicle*'s campaign to keep the Swann Hunter shipyard alive was a case in point; the writing was on the wall but failing to keep fighting on behalf of the region was unthinkable.

Another type of local campaign – the long-term charity fundraiser – is less sexy editorially and demands more time and behind-the-scenes effort than its short, sharp cousin but can often have a bigger and more lasting impact. The *Coventry Telegraph*'s Snowball Appeal is a wonderful example of a long-term force for community good. The appeal, which began in the 1980s, aims to help children who are sick or living with disability by raising money for equipment the NHS cannot provide. Run by a handful of trustees, including the newspaper's editor, the Snowball Appeal has raised a seven-figure sum and helped to improve the lives of thousands of families.

I was so impressed with the Snowball Appeal model that I decided to replicate it in Newcastle. As it happened, the *Chronicle* already had a charity appeal, the Sunshine Fund, founded in 1928 with a donation of £15 from King George V, who had been in the city to open the newly-constructed Tyne Bridge. The fund was launched with the intention of giving underprivileged children a day out at the coast but it had lain dormant for many years until its revival, in its new guise, in the mid-Nineties.

After recruiting a board of trustees, we began to spread the word about the Sunshine Fund. The *Chronicle*'s key role was as the publicity engine, featuring our readers' fundraising events and the families who benefited from their efforts. As in Coventry, it worked a treat. We then decided to launch our own fundraiser, the Sunflower Ball – a black-tie event for 400 guests, with dinner and entertainment.

Since its revival, the Sunshine Fund has gone from strength to strength and, with a staff of five, has become a highly professional operation, which aims to raise £450,000 a year to provide specialised equipment across the

North East for children with disabilities. The Sunflower Ball is now a sparkling highlight of the North East social calendar but I would have to admit that in the early days it occasionally lacked a little polish.

In our second year, the ball was held in a marquee at Newcastle Racecourse, with many of the city's movers and shakers in attendance. I had booked local comedian Dave Johns to compère the event, starting with a short stand-up routine to warm up the audience. A few weeks before the ball, I met Dave – who later starred in the multi-award-winning film *I, Daniel Blake* – to discuss his role as our master of ceremonies. We agreed that, as this was a posh "do" with a mixed audience and several eminent guests, bad language on stage was a no-no.

On the night, Dave got us off to a good start with an amusing welcome speech. He then launched into his stand-up routine, with this gag:

"I went to the hairdresser's the other day. A young lass sat me in the chair. As she's putting the cape on me, she starts chattin'. 'Ee, are yous goin' anywhere nice for ya holidays? I'm thinking of Ibiza but me friend wants to go to Magaluf. I'm not that keen on flying but you have to do it, don't ye?"

*"Then she picks up the scissors and asks me how I'd like me hair cut. I said: 'In complete f****** silence.'"*

My stomach clenched. I scanned the room and noticed the Lady Mayoress and her party sitting stony faced. The Deputy Chief Constable, on the other hand, was rocking with laughter.

But MC Dave dropping the F-bomb was a mere *amuse-bouche* compared with my embarrassment the following year. For the 3rd Sunflower Ball, I set up an organising committee of ten or so *Chronicle* staff, including my new PA, who was given the job of choosing and booking the live entertainment. We began planning well in advance and after a few weeks we had made good progress, but still didn't have the entertainment booked. I felt more relaxed when my PA told me the *Chronicle*'s showbiz editor had recommended an act called Silk Stockings, who had a good reputation across the region.

We agreed that my PA would take in one of their shows, so we could be absolutely sure they were right for our event. The weeks and the planning meetings rolled by. I would ask if she had seen them yet, she would say no, but she'd do it soon. A couple of weeks before our big night, the rule had still not been run over Silk Stockings. But with so little time left, we'd have to go with them, unseen.

One of the cardinal rules of journalism is that you never assume anything. I'd made the mistake of assuming Silk Stockings were a band, and my main concern was that their style of music – whatever it might be – wouldn't sit comfortably with our audience. As the curtain rolled back at the 5-star Gosforth Park Hotel, it was instantly apparent that Silk Stockings were, in fact, a drag duo. Their act was based on miming to big-production numbers, interspersed with risqué, double entendre-laden patter. Their first number drew tepid applause, their second just a thin smattering. This wasn't going well.

Fifteen minutes in and the purpose of the wicker basket they had brought on stage became clear, when one half of the duo reached into it and pulled out a live python. At this point, I was learning how surprisingly quiet 400 people can be.

Paralysed with embarrassment, I shot a glance around my personal guests. The boss of a major construction company and his wife, both regular churchgoers, were open-mouthed. My managing director was eyeballing me, his face contorted in an expression that said: "What the **** were you thinking?". On the next table, my PA had her head in her hands and was sobbing unconsolably. My deputy, meanwhile, had the presence of mind to go backstage and tell Silk Stockings to terminate their act.

In 20 years, this was the first time they'd been hauled off stage, and they weren't happy. You couldn't blame them: they were putting on a show their usual audience loved. The problem was, we'd put them in front of completely the wrong audience. I decided that next year our organising committee of enthusiastic amateurs would have some professional help.

* * * *

It was the morning after the night before – the night of the first Sunflower Ball and my fortieth birthday, to be precise – and I was wrestling an industrial-strength hangover. As I spent a few, quiet moments in my bathroom, with a jackhammer headache for company, my friend and former *Coventry Telegraph* colleague Neil Jagger hollered from downstairs: "Bloody hell, you've been sold!"

The front page of the *Mail on Sunday* business section revealed that Thomson Newspapers, the UK's premier regional publisher and owner of my paper, the *Chronicle*, had agreed to sell most of their titles to Trinity International Holdings. Overnight, the deal would transform Trinity from relative minnow, itself at risk of a takeover as the industry consolidated, into Britain's Number One.

My birthday had been memorable in another, very special way. Before we set off for the ball, my wife Jo had handed me a miniature birthday cake. Where the candle should have been was a pregnancy tester, which showed she was expecting our daughter, Meredith, to add to Joseph, who wasn't yet two, and seven-month-old Rory. On that sunny Sunday morning in rural Northumberland, there was plenty to think about.

Next day, the office was throbbing with gossip. The story goes that the first person in the whole of the Thomson UK business to know about the sale was a print worker in Newcastle, who spotted the headline as the *Mail on Sunday* came off the *Chronicle & Journal* presses, where its Northern editions were printed.

A senior Trinity figure told me later that, such was the scale of the deal, more than 50 of their most trusted staff had been involved in months of detailed background work. All had been sworn to secrecy but the top brass was amazed – and delighted – that nothing had leaked earlier.

In the three months between the MoS's exclusive and the deal being finalised in January 1996, Thomson's granted Trinity limited access to the acquired businesses in Cardiff, Newcastle, Teesside, Belfast and Edinburgh. On their visit to Newcastle, Trinity CEO Philip Graf, finance director Mike Masters and senior executive Stephen Parker were allowed a couple of hours to meet the team and hear a summary of our development plans.

Graf and Parker – who was appointed managing director of the Newcastle business when the deal went through – had spent the early part of their careers with Thomson, so had a good knowledge of what they were buying, and some of the personalities who came with the deal. So, depending on your outlook, this get-to-know-you session had the potential to be either a beauty parade or a firing squad.

A change of ownership is never plain sailing. Those whose careers blossomed under the old regime find their brownie points cancelled and have to start again from scratch. And new owners bring with them their own culture, which may not always be a comfortable fit. For many years, Thomson Newspapers had been regional news publishing's big dog, and they acted like it. Part of an international conglomerate whose other interests included newspapers across the USA and Canada, Thomson Holidays and Britannia Airlines, the company exuded self-confidence and more than a little swagger. They had an excellent reputation and it felt good to work for them.

Trinity was a different proposition, and that was entirely by design. Having learned their trade at Thomson, Graf and Parker knew the best traits of the organisation and they also knew which aspects they didn't like. As a result, Trinity's approach was more understated, less centrally-driven, with more autonomy given to local management. At a get-together for senior staff not long after the takeover, Ulsterman Graf succinctly summarised the Trinity ethos: "We like to win, but not at all costs." It was different, but I liked what I was hearing.

Chapter Fourteen

The Great and the Good

T he higher up journalism's greasy pole you go, the more likely you are to encounter the nation's elite, from business leaders to the political movers and shakers and – every now and then – a member of the nobility.

When I was chosen to meet the Duke of Atholl, on one of his occasional visits to the *Telegraph & Argus*, my instructions from editor Terry Quinn could not have been clearer: "Smile, look interested and don't make an arse of yourself." At least I think he said "arse". It definitely had four letters.

The Eton-educated tenth Duke was chairman of the *T&A*'s parent company Westminster Press, a business previously owned by his grandfather. His duties as chairman took him every now and again to Bradford, York, Oxford, Swindon, Southend, Darlington and other WP publishing centres scattered around the UK. He had inherited the dukedom on the death of either his fourth cousin twice removed or his third cousin three times removed, depending on which of his obituaries you read.

Perks that came with the title included the fairytale castle of Blair, in Perthshire, and 140,000 acres of central Scotland. One of the duke's claims to fame was that he had re-formed the Atholl Highlanders, the last remaining private army in Europe. "You've got so much in common," said the smiling Quinn, "you'll get on like a house on fire."

Wanting to know what to expect, I spoke to a couple of people who had met the Duke on his previous visit. I discovered he had worked in his family printing business, which gave us some sort of shared experience and – bingo! – one of his interests was horse racing.

My opening gambit in our conversation was to ask how his horses were doing, and off he went at a gallop. Nodding at appropriate moments, I managed to get through the next five minutes without embarrassing myself before handing him on to the next person in line. The lunch gathering having passed without an international incident, the Duke took his leave of us. He set off for Bradford train station, an ancient golf bag slung over his shoulder and limping slightly. It was pure P.G. Wodehouse.

And so I'd had my first encounter with the nobility. At least that's what I thought until one of my colleagues revealed to me that Nick Herbert, the charming editorial director of Westminster Press who would pop up to our office from time to time, was in fact Baron Hemingford of Watford.

The first time I met a Prime Minister was in the early part of 1993, at a small, private event for regional editors, held at 10 Downing Street. The format was for the dozen or so editors and a handful of senior civil servants to have a discussion over dinner, with Prime Minister John Major joining us for coffee and an informal, off-the-record Q&A session.

Politically, these were turbulent times and it promised to be an interesting night. After leading his party to a surprise Election victory the previous year, a series of unrelated crises had caused the Prime Minister's popularity, and that of the Government, to slump alarmingly.

Major's problems had started with a storm of protest over pit closures, followed by a sex scandal involving Secretary of State for National Heritage David Mellor. He was then forced to pull Britain out of the European Exchange Rate Mechanism, thereby breaking a manifesto pledge and triggering the financial chaos of Black Wednesday.

The PM then sacked Chancellor Norman Lamont, who took his revenge in his resignation speech, accusing Major of appearing to be "in office but not in power". Within a month, Northern Ireland minister Michael Mates resigned over his links to disgraced businessman Asil Nadir. Mates had given Nadir a watch with the message "Don't let the buggers get you down" engraved on the back, which prompted one of the editors at our dinner to joke that he'd brought a similarly inscribed timepiece for Mr Major.

Some of the veteran editors around the table were accustomed to these events and took the whole thing in their stride. But I confess that my overriding memory of that night was the euphoric feeling that a lad from a Sheffield council estate had been for dinner at No. 10. After the famous black door had closed behind me and I walked along Downing Street towards Whitehall, I couldn't help myself — I did a joyous little jump in the air and clicked my heels together, *à la* Charlie Chaplin. (I know, I know. I just hope they've destroyed the security video).

Of the four Prime Ministers I've met, the most instantly impressive was Tony Blair. The first time I encountered him was at the *Coventry Telegraph*, when he was a shadow minister in Neil Kinnock's Opposition. He was on a visit to the Midlands and, like most politicians of his era, wanted to press the flesh with the local media while he was in town.

Our receptionist called to let me know he and his team had arrived, so I asked her to put them in the lift and I would collect them on the second floor. No sooner had I left my office than Blair came bounding up the stairs, two at a time, his entourage struggling to keep up. As he reached the landing, he was all beaming smile and eye contact. Without breaking his stride, he thrust out his hand and boomed: "Hello, I'm Tony Blair!" It was quite an entrance.

He had a surprisingly good grasp of the key issues in Coventry and managed to appear genuinely interested – a trick some politicians never master, and others don't even attempt. The last time I was in the same room as Blair was at a business awards dinner in Newcastle around 12 years later, towards the end of his time in power. He gave a polished speech but looked tired, drawn and 20 years older. The job had clearly taken its toll.

My other two PMs were Gordon Brown and David Cameron. I met Brown twice – at a Downing Street drinks reception for the regional press and at a private dinner for Trinity Mirror editors. He was serious-minded, earnest and as obviously uncomfortable in those semi-social environments as his reputation suggests.

Cameron was a showman but lacked Blair's high-voltage charisma. At a lunchtime gathering in Westminster for the regional press, the room was abuzz with the news that the police had raided Trinity Mirror's offices that morning, in connection with the phone hacking inquiry. When I was introduced to Cameron, he quipped that there had been "some goings on at your gaff this morning". Your gaff? I hadn't realised Eton was in the East End.

Cameron was our guest at one of a series of lunches hosted by Trinity Mirror chief executive Sly Bailey at our Canary Wharf headquarters. The format was for the visitor – usually a party leader or member of the Cabinet – to set out their political stall for a few minutes as we ate lasagne and fruit salad, followed by a Q&A under Chatham House rules over coffee.

It was my job to invite six or seven of our editors from across the UK and to ensure a representative regional mix. Most of them looked forward to these get-togethers, although one or two saw it more as a duty than a pleasure. I found all of these lunch meetings interesting, in their different ways.

Lib Dem leader Nick Clegg came across as passionate and believable; Chancellor Alastair Darling was warmly human – he had travelled to our offices by Tube rather than in a ministerial car and apologised profusely as he broke off from our discussion to take a call from his teenage son over a minor family crisis; Home Secretary Jacqui Smith seemed totally uninterested, said virtually nothing and couldn't get out of our boardroom quickly enough. Days later, she resigned over her involvement in the MPs' expenses scandal.

Our guests were usually accompanied by one or two advisers; in Cameron's case, it was former Sun editor Andy Coulson, then riding high as Downing Street's director of communications, before his fall from grace over phone hacking. We met them shortly after Cameron's much-derided speech in which he said we should all "hug a hoodie" – a phrase Coulson had dreamed up, which the *Daily Mirror* had branded as "barmy".

A few months later, Sly was invited to bring a handful of her senior regional people to "Dave's gaff" for a working lunch. I met the editors of five of our largest titles at the St Stephen's Tavern, across the road from Downing Street, so we could arrive at No.10 together.

We entered the PM's office to find the lunch that had been prepared reflected the Cameron-Osborne era of austerity we were now living in. There were two small plates of finger-thin sandwiches, with the crusts removed, and a slice of fruit cake, cut into several tiny portions. Each of us took a single sliver of sandwich and did the mental maths to calculate whether there was enough cake to go round.

The flagship policy of Cameron's 2010 election campaign was the Big Society, which envisaged a Britain in which power was taken away from politicians and handed to local people and communities. The problem was that, when it came to implementation, Dave's big idea was gaining little traction, possibly because its success depended on community volunteering on a scale never before seen in Britain and – realistically – never likely to happen. It was a nice idea that would never fly. Nevertheless, he gave us the hard sell, urging the editors of these influential regional titles to get behind the Big Society.

When the editors expressed their unanimous view that the project wouldn't work unless real money was put behind it, Cameron became tetchy. He lectured us about his great scheme and why we should all back it. I could sense the editors' brains switching to sleep mode.

We emerged from No. 10 to find a gleaming, black limousine waiting to whisk Sly back to Canary Wharf, where it would appear the cold wind of austerity had yet to be felt. She stopped for a second and smiled for the Downing Street paparazzi before hopping in. The editors and I laughed about our lightweight lunch as we wandered back to the St Stephen's Tavern, which I can confirm does a passable pie and chips.

* * * *

Over the years, I've met various members of the House of Windsor. To be precise, one Queen, three Princes and a Princess*. I found all of these encounters fascinating but one of them, unfortunately, was the precursor to a quite stomach-churning incident.

With accidental good timing, Jo and I were invited to a Buckingham Palace garden party which was to take place on the day of our tenth wedding anniversary. We decided to make a special trip of it, so I booked us in at a Mayfair hotel and lined up a couple of surprise, *après* garden party treats.

The weather on the day was glorious, with endless blue sky and the mercury nudging the 90s. As the sun beat down, we ate dainty sandwiches and cakes, and drank tea from bone china cups. It was a lovely way to spend an afternoon. After a delightful walk around the palace gardens, we decamped to the Ritz Hotel's Rivoli Bar, for a celebratory bottle of champagne and some posh snacks. From there, we headed to Claridge's Hotel for a delicious dinner in the Gordon Ramsay restaurant. It was a perfect day.

The next morning, we hopped on to our north-bound train at Euston feeling relaxed and happy. But soon after we arrived home, the trouble started. I began to feel queasy and before long was violently ill. Aching from head to foot and feeling utterly drained, I took to my bed. I stayed there for the next four days, shivering uncontrollably, my stomach doing somersaults. Eventually, we called a doctor.

*Queen Elizabeth II, Princes Philip, Charles and Andrew, and Princess Margaret.

He organised some tests, which showed I had been laid low by campylobacter, a nasty form of food poisoning. The doctor prescribed antibiotics and gave me a green form to be sent to my local hospital, on which I had to list all the places I had eaten in the 72 hours before I'd been taken ill. Presumably, the person who received it thought they had a joker on their hands when they read: "Buckingham Palace, The Ritz and Claridge's". I never heard back from them.

A few years later, I was in the presence of the Queen again, this time at a summer reception for the media, held at Windsor Castle. The Royal Family turned out in force, as did a wealth of media "royalty".

Before our hosts arrived, we were given a short briefing on protocol ("Call her Ma'am, rhymes with ham") and were told to arrange ourselves in groups of six, forming a shallow semi-circle to facilitate the Royal mingling. In my group were a couple of national editors and three from regionals, including Paul 'Tigger' Thomas, editor of the *Windsor, Slough & Eton Express*, who enjoyed pointing out to the other guests: "It's the Queen's local paper".

As we waited for the Royal party to enter the room, Paul told us Her Majesty was an avid reader of his paper, and that if a production problem ever delayed delivery, a member of staff from Windsor Castle would soon be on the phone, asking when they might expect their copies to arrive. I'm sure one or two of his fellow editors wrote this off as a bit of editorial *braggadocio*.

Eventually, the Queen arrived at our group and, ignoring the big-hitters, made a beeline for Paul. "Ah, Mr Thomas, I've been wanting to speak to you …'"and she launched into an animated discussion about a story in that week's edition. One nil to the little guy.

Chapter Fifteen

Fifty Thousand Hopeful Zebras

From the newspaper perspective, there's only one sport that counts, and that's football. And there are very few places where it counts more than in Newcastle-upon-Tyne.

I had the great good luck to join the *Evening Chronicle* as editor around three weeks into Newcastle United's first season in the Premier League. Kevin Keegan, revered by fans for his stellar performances for the Toon in the twilight of his playing career, had returned as manager two seasons previously, with the club facing relegation to the third tier for the first time in their history. That would almost certainly have put them out of business. In his first season, he saved them from the drop. In his second, they were promoted as champions, playing an irresistible brand of attacking football that overwhelmed their opponents, week after week.

Over the summer of 1993, as I worked my notice at the *Coventry Evening Telegraph*, I couldn't wait to make a start at the *Chronicle*, a Top Ten regional title. Before being interviewed for the job, I'd never been to Newcastle, so to get to know the paper and the city, I had a copy sent to me in Coventry every day.

As the summer wore on, I became concerned that the paper had too much football in it. There was understandable anticipation about their debut in the Premier League but here we were in the heart of the off-season and the paper was gorging on football. The sports pages were full of it, as you might expect, but so too were the news and features sections. Sorting this out would be my number one priority.

Arriving for my first day at the *Chronicle* offices in Groat Market, I got into the lift with a young woman who I guessed was an advertising rep. She was beaming from ear to ear. "Ee, did you see the match? Weren't they great?" She had no idea who I was, and she didn't care. She simply couldn't contain her excitement at Newcastle's win the previous day.

It was the same story on the editorial floor; gnarled, seen-it-all journalists were wreathed in smiles. After dropping my coat in my new office, I went upstairs to see managing director Tony Hill. His PA welcomed me to the company and immediately set off on a eulogy about Keegan, the club and the players. The whole building was buzzing. I'd never known anything like it. After approximately half an hour in my new job, I decided it was impossible for the *Chronicle* to have too much football.

Despite the euphoria gripping the city, my first visit to St James's Park left a bitter taste. On a dripping wet October night, the Toon were hosting my team, Sheffield Wednesday. It all started out so well for the Owls – inspired by former England star Chris Waddle, they led 2-1 with less than 15 minutes to play. A win for the visitors seemed nailed on. Then, in a foretaste of many memorable games to come, Newcastle tore up the script. Andrew Cole equalised and, five minutes later, substitute Alex Mathie – in his only memorable contribution to the Toon cause – scored a wonder goal. Two minutes before full-time, Newcastle scored their fourth to seal an outrageous win.

In the seasons that followed, glorious victories, improbable comebacks and the occasional heartbreak came as standard with Newcastle United. And after 30 years of the dismal fare served up at Hillsborough, I was hooked on the technicolour football of the men in black and white stripes.

A few weeks after the Sheffield Wednesday drubbing, I was invited for a get-to-know-you lunch at Newcastle Breweries by managing director Alastair Wilson and marketing director Jim Merrington. Alastair, an affable Scot who would later serve as communications director at Newcastle United, summed up my new city in a single sentence: "There are four brands that matter to the people of Newcastle – the Tyne Bridge, the football club, Brown Ale and the *Chronicle*." It was an astute observation, which spawned a series of successful collaborations between NUFC, the brewery and the newspaper.

The first was the launch of a Player of the Month competition, promoted through the *Chronicle*. Readers who voted for the winner went into a draw and a lucky dozen would be invited to a buffet lunch at the brewery's visitor centre, opposite St James' Park, where they would rub shoulders with the players. The success of the event was largely down to Keegan, who insisted the whole first team squad would attend the lunch, without fail. This gave a small band of our readers one of the most memorable days of their lives and provided the *Chronicle* with some good content and a great deal of goodwill.

As Keegan's newly-promoted Entertainers wowed fans all over the country, they were supported by an equally formidable back-room team. Chairman Sir John Hall, who had made his name and his fortune by building the MetroCentre, one of the UK's first out-of-town shopping malls, had a North East native's understanding of the Geordie in the street. One of his shrewdest and most crowd-pleasing acts after winning control following a bitter takeover battle had been to appoint Keegan as manager, sparking the on-field revival, rekindling the interest of fans and – crucially – boosting gate receipts.

The extra cash at the turnstiles and Hall's property development expertise combined to turn St James's Park from a drab, decaying, out-of-date hulk into a modern, 52,000-seat stadium that would become the jewel in the Newcastle city centre skyline. The original plan involved moving the ground to a new site on the nearby Leazes Park, and to create a sporting club modelled on Milan's San Siro, but it was rejected by the city's planners. Not a man to be easily deterred, Hall decided to demolish the existing stands and to build taller replacements with many more seats, bar areas and new executive boxes.

To boost the ground capacity further, the four open corners were filled in with extra seating, but this caused an unexpected problem; the wind could no longer provide a natural draught to dry the pitch, causing it to cut up badly every time it was played on. Keegan cut up rough, too, demanding a better surface to suit his team's fluent style of play. The pitch was re-laid a number of times before a solution was found. Between matches, a set of specially-designed, high-powered heaters was wheeled out and directed at the pitch, to do the job that Mother Nature had previously done for free.

Freddie Fletcher, a streetwise Scot who had transformed Glasgow Rangers commercially, was recruited by Hall as chief executive, with a brief to unlock the sleeping Tyneside giant's money-making potential. In a candid one-to-one discussion at the ground, Fletcher opened up to me about the previous regime's lack of commercial acumen. Referring to them dismissively as The Blazers, he said: "They even lost money on the club lottery. That's almost impossible to do, but they managed it."

Unfortunately for me and the *Chronicle*, Fletcher's eye for an opportunity led him to poach one of my best photographers, Ian Horrocks, to be the club's first official cameraman. Looking back, this was an early example of Premier League clubs seeking to control and commercialise their own media output, breaking up the symbiotic – some would say cosy – relationships built up over many years with the local press.

Riding high in the Premier League and feeding off the enthusiasm across the city, the club was full of ambition. One of Fletcher's priorities was to make more use of the revamped stadium, which was packed for two and a half hours on match days, with the tills ringing, but lay dormant the rest of the week. One of his first ideas was decidedly off-the-wall – a fashion show.

In the summer of 1995, Fletcher had made five significant signings: French international winger David Ginola, striker Les Ferdinand, goalkeeper Shaka Hislop, full-back Warren Barton and fashion designer George Davis. The man behind Next and George at Asda had been brought in to create a clothing range for the club. Now for the clever bit – Fletcher wanted to pull all of this together in a fashion show at the ground, with the four new players among the catwalk models. The *Chronicle*'s role was to promote the show and drive ticket applications. On a September evening, with the Gallowgate end almost full and the London media attending in force, Fletcher was a happy man.

Although the club's commercial trajectory as a whole was on rocket-boosters, they did experience the occasional misfire. In November 1995, as part of his mission to sweat the stadium asset, Fletcher opened a high-end restaurant, named the Magpie Room, with respected local chef John Blackmore running the kitchen.

The official opening was perfectly timed, with Keegan's team sitting proudly on top of the Premier League. Actress Denise Welch, who was starring in TV's *Soldier, Soldier* at the time, and her husband Tim Healy, of *Auf Wiedersehen, Pet* fame, were among the Tyneside "royalty" in attendance. Sir John Hall proudly revealed a specially-commissioned painting of two fighting magpies by French artist Henri Bismuth as the visual centrepiece of the restaurant.

One of the Magpie Room's unique selling points was its commanding views, with the lights of the city centre shimmering to the South and the stadium itself looking a picture through the floor-to-ceiling restaurant windows. Diners had the option of taking their after-dinner coffee in the new stand where they could drink in the atmosphere of the silent stadium. By night, under floodlights, it had a strangely magical quality. But while the Magpie Room appeared to have all the right ingredients, it never found the recipe for commercial success. A few years later, the space it occupied was turned into a match-day bar.

At Newcastle Breweries, the marketing team were always looking to add interest to the Player of the Month event by introducing extra elements that would make good pictures. On one occasion, they arranged for members of a local Army regiment, just back from a tour in Northern Ireland, to join us for lunch.

The soldiers, in full uniform, looked magnificent – none more so than a very large sergeant whose beret had an eye-catching thistle at the front. Coincidentally, star winger Ginola had arrived at the lunch sporting a natty, navy-blue beret. As we lined up for the customary group photo, Ginola suggested they swap headgear. The sergeant agreed and, just as the shutter clicked, Ginola shot a cheeky look at the towering soldier. The picture was published in newspapers and magazines all over the world.

If Ginola's swashbuckling performances on the pitch made him a hit with the fans, his flowing mane and Gallic good looks established him as a heartthrob among the womenfolk of Tyneside. As part of our annual sponsorship package, the *Chronicle* could invite 50 guests to one of the choicest Newcastle home fixtures. With managing director Tony Hill away on holiday, it fell to me to host the Newcastle v Arsenal game on January 2, 1996, and to present the man of the match award in the sponsor's lounge afterwards.

The game was one minute old when Ginola picked up the ball on the left and set off on a slaloming run, leaving bewildered Arsenal defenders in his wake. Nearing the corner of the penalty area, he cut inside and unleashed a right-foot shot which curled unstoppably into the top corner. As the crowd erupted, my wife Jo turned to me and whispered: "If Peter Beardsley wins man of the match, you can present it to him. If it's Ginola, I'm doing it." It was, and she did.

Having borne the burden of supporting Sheffield Wednesday for 30 arid years, the games at St James' Park during this golden period made the heart sing. There were many memorable matches: a 7-1 trouncing of Spurs; an Andy Cole hat-trick in a 3-0 win in the snow against Liverpool (when the second goal went in, the roar of the crowd was so loud it blew out the speakers in the Newcastle Breweries box); and a 6-1 battering of Wimbledon, in which Vinnie Jones ended the game as an emergency goalkeeper. As he donned the gloves, the Newcastle fans in the Gallowgate end greeted him with a chant of: "Dodgy keeper!" A couple of minutes later, after he made a decent save, the chant changed to: "Super keeper!", much to Vinnie's amusement.

Among all these memories, there are two matches, in particular, that stand out. The first was the 5-0 annihilation of Manchester United, where Newcastle achieved a degree of redemption after conceding the Premier League title to Alex Ferguson's team the previous season, following Keegan's "I'd love it" meltdown. On a day when everything Newcastle touched turned to goals, Jo and I were guests of Barclays, the club's bankers. Half an hour or so after the final whistle, a beaming Freddie Fletcher arrived in the Barclays box and invited the remaining handful of us to have a drink with him in the directors' lounge.

As we made our way through the bowels of the stadium, striker Ferdinand – one of Newcastle's scorers – was walking towards us. Wearing a dark grey suit and a white, open-necked shirt, he looked like a god. Just as our paths crossed, Jo – a few drinks to the good and still giddy from her Ginola encounter a few months earlier – decided to engage him with a few well-chosen words. "Ooh, Les," she said, "you … you … you lovely man." Ferdinand flashed her a killer smile and, wisely, continued on his way.

We arrived at the directors' lounge and standing by the door was a glum-looking chap in a grey overcoat and a flat cap, waiting for his lift back to Manchester. It hadn't been the happiest of afternoons for Sir Bobby Charlton.

My second extra-special moment happened on a monsoon-wet Tuesday night in February 1999, when Newcastle entertained Coventry City – a mid-table clash and far from the most glamorous fixture in the Premier League calendar. Newcastle conceded an early goal but came back to win 4-1 in a match with little at stake. This was the first time I took my sons, Joe and Rory to a game. They were aged six and four. The roar that greeted the team as they ran on to the pitch hit my boys like a bolt of lightning, jolting them upright in their seats. From that moment, they were Toon fans.

* * * *

All the on-field drama of the Keegan years was eclipsed by one sensational off-the-field event – the signing of Alan Shearer. For Newcastle fans, Tuesday, July 30, 1996, is the equivalent of the first Moon landing. Everyone knows where they were when it happened. In my case, it was my mother-in-law's back garden in Lincolnshire.

138

On a sunny morning, I was playing with the kids when my mobile rang; it was *Chronicle* assistant editor Roger Borrell. He apologised for interrupting my holiday but he thought I'd want to know that Shearer had just been signed for a world record fee of £15 million. The first team squad was in Hong Kong on a pre-season tour when Keegan took the *Chronicle*'s Alan Oliver and his counterpart from the *South Shields Gazette* to one side and gave them the biggest exclusive of their careers.

It was a story that editors dream of but rather than call the shots from 150 miles down the A1, I felt Roger and the team should have their day. I wished him all the best and went back to pushing the children's swing. The *Chronicle* team produced an outstanding front page, with Shearer pictured in action, wearing the famous black-and-white stripes. It was a neat piece of Photoshop work, with Shearer's head grafted on to midfielder Rob Lee's body. Sales went berserk.

During those tumultuous years on Tyneside, we shared many high points with the club. But every now and then the relationship would hit choppy waters. One Monday morning, chairman Sir John Hall called me to discuss a story we were planning to run in that day's edition. The team had played a Premier League game on the south coast over the weekend, but the big news had nothing to do with the action on the pitch. Club captain Barry Venison had ducked out of a ten-pin bowling trip, organised by Keegan to pass the time before following day's match, and spent the afternoon in the hotel bar with two younger players. A furious Keegan promptly stripped Venison of the captaincy and told him he wouldn't be playing the next day.

Sir John had heard that we had the story and called me to ask if we were planning to publish it. I told him we were, and why: the fans would want to know why Venison hadn't played; at the next home game everyone would see he was no longer wearing the captain's armband; and – above all – it was a great story.

Sir John asked how much prominence we planned to give the article and I told him it was the main story on our back page. He went quiet and I could sense his brow furrowing. I explained we'd been all set to splash the Keegan-Venison bust-up on the front page until we heard there had been a triple murder in Gateshead that morning. It was quite a news day.

On another occasion, my managing director Stephen Parker was summoned to St James's Park following the publication of a story in the

Chronicle's stablemate the *Sunday Sun*. A double-page spread had been given over to a sequence of aerial photographs showing Kevin Keegan's sumptuous house on Sir John Hall's Wynyard Hall Estate, with arrows highlighting where some of the main rooms were situated. Although my remit didn't extend to the *Sunday Sun*, Stephen took me along as our editorial spokesman. We were accompanied by our finance director John Williams, for reasons which still escape me.

Keegan's mood was somewhere between livid and apoplectic, and he turned the verbal flamethrower on us. Chief executive Fletcher and Sir John Hall's son Douglas, a director of the club, sat silently as KK let rip. This was particularly difficult for Stephen – a lifelong Liverpool fan for whom Keegan was a footballing hero. We tried to explain the rationale for the story but anything we said served only to make matters worse. Still seething, Keegan left the room.

If we thought the temperature would cool, it didn't. Fletcher and Hall took up where the manager had left off. Hall demanded an apology from us; we said we stood by the story. After a few minutes of stalemate, Stephen, searching for some middle ground, said we were sorry the story had offended the manager and offered to write to the club to that effect. This was deemed acceptable by Hall and Fletcher but a few days later, presumably after they had discussed the letter with Keegan, word reached us that they were still unhappy with what they saw as a qualified apology.

Nonetheless, after a few frosty weeks, something close to normal service was resumed – an indication that, despite their annoyance at this particular story, the club appreciated the value of their relationship with Newcastle Chronicle & Journal Ltd.

At the time, we felt we were within our rights to publish the pictures, but I suspect the press regulator might take a different view if the same pictures were published today. Over the years, the regulatory framework that news publishers work within has become steadily more rigorous and, despite what the keyboard warriors say, modern-day editors take care to balance the individual's right to privacy with the public's right to know.

A couple of years after the Keegan firestorm, I attended another feisty meeting at St James' Park with his successor Kenny Dalglish. Keegan had resigned, feeling he had taken the club as far as he could, and the board needed a big name to replace him. They had landed one of the very biggest in Liverpool legend Dalglish.

But the early gloss soon wore off; the fans were unhappy with the style of football being played, and Dalglish was unhappy with the way the *Chronicle* was reporting it. Matters came to a head after a home defeat and an insipid performance, which the *Chronicle*'s back-page banner headline described as "GUTLESS".

Also at the meeting were Dalglish's assistant Terry McDermott and Alan Shearer, who was representing the players, while the away team comprised *Chronicle* editor Alison Hastings, sports editor Paul New and me, in my new role as editor-in-chief of the *Evening Chronicle* and its sister morning paper *The Journal*. We were ushered into the manager's office, where we found Dalglish leaning back in his chair, his shoeless feet resting on an open desk drawer. He zeroed in on one of our reports that had offended him. When we disputed his interpretation of the piece, he halted the meeting and demanded the cutting be faxed over from our office. After a few awkwardly silent minutes, the fax finally dropped. We were proved to be right but Dalglish immediately moved on another story he didn't like but which was also factually correct. Eventually, he found a piece that we agreed contained an error. We were bang to rights, apparently.

Next came the thorny issue of player ratings or "match marks" as we called them in the paper. The players absolutely detest them, said Dalglish. He was right, they do – especially if their latest performance was rated a five out of ten. (The *Chronicle*'s unwritten rule at the time was that five is as low as you go). Interestingly, when Dalglish invited Shearer to jump in on this subject, he didn't push it hard. Then again, when you're getting nines and tens every week …

The meeting ended with the *Chronicle* team holding our ground and Dalglish still far from happy. A couple of weeks later, the situation deteriorated further when another article prompted him to call our Newcastle United reporter Alan Oliver, to express his displeasure.

Later that season, for the first and only time, the Newcastle manager gave an in-depth interview to the city's Metro Radio station. The content wasn't earth-shattering but Metro ran it over two or three nights, quite rightly milking their exclusive for all it was worth. It was a coup for them and a poke in the eye for us. We realised then that the days of partnership and world exclusives were over.

Keegan's Entertainers never won a major trophy, but they achieved legendary status among the fans and their era is seen as one of the highest points in the club's history. Their legacy? A constant longing among Newcastle fans for a team of similar quality, playing the same daredevil way.

A few years ago, a national newspaper journalist described the St James's Park crowd, decked out in their black-and-white striped replica shirts and yearning for success, as fifty thousand hopeful zebras. They say in football it's the hope that kills you, and in the 14 miserable years of Mike Ashley's ownership the club, the fans' hopes were slowly strangled.

Of course, Newcastle's new Saudi owners bring with them their own brand of controversy, focused principally on the kingdom's human rights record. But for the long-suffering supporters of this historic club, the change of ownership revives their dreams of better footballing days ahead. I hope those dreams are realised.

Chapter Sixteen

To the Dark Side ... and Back

L ife as an editor has several parallels with football management. You are responsible for getting the best out of a team of talented and often free-spirited individuals, some of whom quite enjoy making life difficult for you. And the work you do is on show for everyone to see and criticise – a right that some choose to exercise loudly and publicly.

A finance director I used to work with would occasionally voice his opinions on the paper's shortcomings in front of the full senior management team. He would always preface his comments with "Speaking as a reader ...", which he felt gave him the right to hold forth on everything from the choice of front-page splash to the use of colour panels on Page 37. Of course, he was entitled to his view. But I imagine he wouldn't have been too happy if I had wandered into the accounts department and publicly rubbished his team's double-entry book-keeping.

Another of our finance chiefs was "speaking as a reader" when he opined that one of the titles in our wider group was far brighter looking than another title published in a different part of the country. This drabness must mean something was going wrong editorially, and was therefore the editor's fault.

The main difference was that the "bright" title was printed on a modern press that delivered sharp reproduction and full colour on every page, while the "drab" one was printed on a creaky old machine with muddy reproduction and colour available on just one page in eight. My suggestion that the group might want to brighten up the drab title by investing a few million in a new press fell on deaf ears. This sort of public rock-throwing can be irritating for the editor, especially when it comes from within the business, but as time goes by you learn to accept that it comes with the territory.

Another similarity with football management is that an editor's professional life-expectancy can be relatively short. It seems unlikely that today's incumbents or those who follow them are likely to enjoy the longevity in their respective hot seats of Sir Alex Ferguson at Manchester United or Paul Dacre at the *Daily Mail*. But back in pre-Internet days, the editor's lifespan was often 20 years plus, which could create its own problems. Some editors

I knew had stayed in one place too long, and they, their staff and their papers had grown stale together.

Before I became an editor, I was mulling over the idea of moving into general management at some point. With luck, I reckoned I could make it to the editor's chair by my late 30s. But it wouldn't be good for the newspaper or the business if I was still there come retirement. Even if I moved to a new title for a fresh challenge, did I want to simply replay my greatest hits to a new audience, as I had seen others do?

So when the opportunity to become managing director at the Gazette Media Company presented itself, I grabbed it. By then I had edited two papers and dipped my toes into a more commercial role, leading a web development team. The time felt right to take the plunge into general management. Or, as one of my fellow editors put it, going over to the Dark Side.

With a staff of more than 400 and a turnover of £20 million, the Middlesbrough-based *Gazette* was a meaningful business within the parent company and the region. Shortly before I took up my new role, a contact in Newcastle rang to congratulate me and said: "You're a businessman now." I half-expected him to add: "So you'll need to start behaving like a grown-up." I was delighted to have been promoted but there was also a feeling of loss. I had always been proud to call myself a journalist, to be an outsider, a fly on the wall. How would I adjust to life as a "suit"?

From the outset, the Teesside business community made me feel extremely welcome. The *Gazette* – like most local and regional titles – was front and centre in the life of the area, and the managing director was, *de facto*, a key player. My predecessor Steve Brown, who was leaving Teesside to run the bigger business in Newcastle, told me the difference between the two places was that Newcastle has all the benefits of being the regional capital (with no major city for 100 miles to the north or south), while on Teesside, nothing comes for free. "You have to chisel it out."

With its heavy-industrial backdrop – the inspiration for the post-apocalyptic imagery of Ridley Scott's Blade Runner – Middlesbrough is never going to win a best-in-show rosette. It's development in recent years has been hampered by the decline of its traditional industries and its geography; the town is out on a limb, 15 miles from the East Coast main line and half-an-hour's drive from the arterial motorway network. It's a gritty place, with gritty inhabitants who don't hold back from criticising their home town, but if they hear an outsider saying a harsh word, you'd better reach for your tin hat.

One grey winter's morning, I was visited by a consultant from McKinsey, who were doing some strategy work for our parent group. She had travelled up from London, and it hadn't been the smoothest journey. For the final leg from Middlesbrough station to the *Gazette* office, she had taken a cab. They say taxi drivers can be the best advertisement for any town; they are often the first person a visitor encounters and they create an instant first impression of the place. My visitor's cabbie struck up a conversation by asking where she had come from. "London," she said. "Hmmm, London. So why the f*** have you come to this dump?" I've never understood why the council didn't adopt that as its marketing slogan.

The *Gazette* offices in Borough Road were a local landmark, as was the phone box immediately outside. It was a social hub of sorts, where drug deals were done and sex was paid for, and sometimes performed. On one memorable day, three police cars swooped to arrest those inside, as the *Gazette*'s journalists looked on from the newsroom windows.

For me, the best part of being an MD was having the opportunity to build my own senior management team, and in my first few months I recruited an advertising director and an editor, the two key roles at any newspaper. The latter was always going to be the trickier appointment. How would potential editors feel about having an editorial man as their boss? How involved did I intend to be in editorial matters? The response to the job advertisement was exceptionally strong, so I decided to concentrate on making the very best appointment I could, and to let the new editor get on with it, with no interference from me.

The one time I did get involved in editorial at the *Gazette* was when I brought in a story – and it was a pretty good one. Jo and I had set up home in a village south of Middlesbrough, attracted by the local school, which was one of the top 20 state primaries in the *Sunday Times*' annual list, based on its pupils' performance in the Standard Assessment Tests. We lived just outside its catchment area but after pleading our case to the governors, and with support from headteacher, our three children were accepted. It seemed a happy place, in an idyllic spot, overlooked by the imposing North York Moors. We couldn't have been more pleased.

But within a few weeks of the children starting at the school, we began to have concerns. When we asked: "What did you do today?" the kids would say "not much" or that school had been boring. This was very different from their previous school, where they had been engaged and excited. Maybe things would improve after a few weeks, when they had settled in. But things didn't improve, and we became increasingly puzzled by the apparent discrepancy between the outstanding test results and the education our children were receiving.

A couple of terms in, the governors sent a letter to all parents, telling us the head had been suspended following allegations of irregularities in the SATs. The gossip at the school gate was that children had been given extra time or were told they might want to try answering this or that question again. So the test results, which had made the school so attractive to us and other parents, couldn't be trusted.

I tipped off the *Evening Gazette* newsdesk and the story was splashed on the front-page of the next edition. The governors then sent out another letter, urging parents not to speak to the press. Some parents defended the head, saying that in similar circumstances they would want their child to be given extra help (which would extend, presumably, to their GCSEs, A levels, university finals and their driving test). A few weeks later, after an investigation by the local education authority and the school governors, the headteacher resigned.

It turned out that our head was not alone. In the year 2000, 147 headteachers across the country faced allegations of test-fixing, which David Hart, general secretary of the headteachers' union the NAHT, said was fuelled by the pressure of performance targets and performance-related pay.

* * * *

Certain aspects of a life as a managing director were great. I loved the people side of the business – communicating with staff, developing their skills, creating a sense of togetherness and shared purpose. Other parts I found terminally dull. Try as I might, I couldn't drum up any interest as the advertising director explained to me in fine detail why the revenue yield in the Motors category had been marginally short of target the previous Tuesday.

So here I was in my mid-40s, with the prospect of 20 years in general management ahead of me, and I wasn't particularly enjoying my job. It was a demanding role and I was always fully occupied, but I was missing the buzz of journalism. Some time earlier, my boss in Newcastle had asked me why more editors didn't become MDs. Now I knew. It just wasn't as much fun. But I'd made my move and was prepared to dig in for the long haul – until regionals' boss Stephen Parker lobbed a hand grenade into our monthly MDs meeting.

Just before we broke for lunch, he announced that he planned to appoint an editorial director for Trinity's 100-plus regional titles. This was a fundamental change of policy for the company, whose frequently-expressed view was that local editors knew their markets best and should be allowed to get on with editing, untroubled by interfering know-alls from "Group". Curiously, that same belief didn't apply to the advertising department, where there was a well-established group commercial director.

The announcement was greeted with stunned silence by the dozen or so of us around the boardroom table, but minds were racing – the other local MDs wondering if their leader had developed a drug habit, while I was weighing up the best time to ask / demand that he give me the job.

"Shy bairns get nowt", as they say in the North East, so at the close of the day's business I collared Stephen and told him I wanted to be his editorial director. "Why?" he asked. "Because I think I'd do it well. And because I couldn't bear it if you appointed somebody else and they screwed it up." Stephen asked me to write to him, outlining how I saw the role. I didn't realise it at the time, but I was being asked to write my own job description.

* * * *

Four months into my new job, I drove to Howden, in east Yorkshire, to meet Press Association chief executive Paul Potts, who had invited me for a tour of their new northern production base.

When I started my career at *The Star*, Potts was the paper's ace local government reporter. As a naive newcomer, I marvelled at his ability to produce a seemingly endless stream of front-page exclusives, which he would bash out ferociously on a typewriter dating from the early Cretaceous period. Now, he was the boss of Britain's national news agency and I was the newly-appointed editorial chief of the country's leading regional newspaper group (and PA's biggest shareholder), so it was a priority for both of us that this relationship should work.

Howden is a small market town in the Vale of York, 37 miles from Leeds and 30 miles from Hull. It's close to the M62 and M18 motorways but the vast majority of drivers don't bother making the short detour to the town. If they did, they'd find a beautiful medieval minster, some interesting independent shops and a couple of pubs that do a decent lunch. It's a quiet backwater, and at first pass it doesn't look the sort of place you'd choose to build a major production hub serving the UK's print media.

But Potts had spotted three big advantages in creating PA's new base here. First, substantial grants were on offer to employers who brought jobs to the area. Secondly, there was a surprisingly large talent pool to tap into. The town's position adjacent to the motorway network made it commutable for a large number of experienced sub-editors living on Humberside and in the West Yorkshire and South Yorkshire conurbations, who could take a job with PA without needing to uproot their families.

Thirdly, although the pay on offer at Howden compared favourably with most newspapers in the North, it was significantly lower than the going rate in London. Taken together, these three factors made the financial case a slam-dunk. Within a couple of years, Potts's new production centre had become the biggest employer in the area, giving Howden a significant economic boost.

The set-up at PA was impressive; they had been quick to realise the potential of automated content - particularly in data-heavy material such as sports results and TV listings - which made their editorial process highly efficient and extremely low cost.

They also pioneered some innovative content-gathering processes, for example employing former professional footballers* to attend games from where they would text a simple description of the action – "Corner to United on the left. Rovers' goalkeeper saves" – into PA's databases. This provided the raw material for some of the earliest computer-generated match reports.

Many old pros whose careers had ended before the big money flooded into football were grateful for a regular, football-related earner.

After a tour of the offices, Potts and I sat down with his commercial director Marc Tucker for a buffet lunch in the boardroom. We had barely filled our plates when there was a knock at the door and Potts's secretary walked in. She apologised for interrupting but she thought we'd want to know that a plane had just hit the World Trade Centre.

We sat silently for a moment. Our journalistic instincts were jangling while our business brains told us to stay put; we were here to initiate an important working relationship, and the contracts we would be discussing were worth a seven-figure sum.

Potts said his news team didn't need him to be involved and, anyway, they wouldn't thank him for poking his nose in. I was in a similar boat – as Trinity Mirror's editorial director, I was responsible for the development of more than 100 titles, but day-to-day decisions on content were, firmly, the job of our editors. We resumed our lunch and our business discussion.

Minutes later, there was another knock at the door. A second airliner had flown into the South tower. What we had initially assumed to be a tragic accident was obviously something far more sinister. Lunch was abandoned. After a hasty goodbye, Potts hared off to the newsroom while I got into my car. I called Jo, who was at home and unaware of the unfolding horror. I told her she should switch on the TV.

For two hours as I drove back, she relayed the news as it broke. A third plane had hit the Pentagon. A fourth had crashed into a field in Pennsylvania. Office workers, faced with the inferno ripping through the Twin Towers, were leaping from the windows and hurtling 1,000 feet or more to certain death. By the time I arrived home, both towers had collapsed, their metal ribs sticking in the air like an antelope picked clean by vultures.

In an immediate response to the shocking events unfolding in America, several high-profile London buildings were evacuated, for fear that terrorists might launch similar attacks on the UK. Among them was One Canada Square, the Canary Wharf business district's iconic skyscraper where Trinity Mirror's corporate HQ was housed.

Before 9/11, I never gave it a second thought as plane after plane took off from nearby City Airport and made a beeline for our building before turning right or left on to its flight path. In the months after the attacks, I felt a chill of apprehension every time I looked out from the 21st floor windows and saw a plane heading straight towards us.

* * * *

Summed up in a sentence, my role as editorial director was to use the scale of Britain's biggest regional publisher to improve our products, drive down costs, develop our staff and create a stronger team ethic. Before 2001, the business had been a series of individual fiefdoms, each ruled by a local managing director and an editor, who were used to being top dogs. Convincing them to change the habits of a lifetime wouldn't be straightforward.

One of my first decisions as editorial director was to introduce a quarterly meeting of our senior editors. It doubled as a bonding exercise and a forum for us to discuss a wide range of editorial topics – some of which the editors found more engaging than others. When we talked about content, their ears invariably pricked up. But when I raised thornier issues, such as sharing production facilities or the need to find budget savings, the reception could be a little cooler. Aware that these meetings could be heavy going, I tried to leaven the mix inviting an external guest or two.

In the summer of 2005, we met in Canary Wharf for what proved to be one of our most memorable get-togethers. Our guests were Esther Rantzen, in her role as founder of Childline, who I had agreed we would partner in an awareness drive, subject to the editors' sign-off; and Dianne Thompson, chief executive of Camelot, the company behind the National Lottery, and a long-term supporter of both the regional press and the UK's Olympic teams. Before giving her presentation, Dianne confided that she was feeling nervous, as the International Olympic Committee's decision on who would host the 2012 Games was due at any moment.

Esther's nerves were a little frayed too. Against her assistant's advice, she had decided she would drive herself to Canary Wharf but as the clock ticked towards her slot on the agenda, there was no sign of our star guest. Her assistant then fielded the first of several calls from an increasingly flustered Esther, who had spent 20 minutes cruising the concrete canyons, unable to find the car park. Eventually, her assistant talked her in and she arrived at our offices, full of apologies and obviously stressed.

She took a minute or two to compose herself but as I stood up to introduce her, she still seemed disorientated and I feared the worst. I needn't have worried. As I handed over to her, she perched herself on the edge of a desk, flashed a 1,000-megawatt smile and delivered an impassioned appeal – delivered effortlessly and without notes – imploring the editors to support Childline. From the first moment, she had the audience in the palm of her hand, and they couldn't sign up quickly enough.

Esther's bravura performance had barely ended when Dianne Thompson screamed from the back of the room: "We've won the Olympics!", sending an electric buzz of excitement through the room. As the meeting ended and I joined the throngs of commuters heading home, the nation was beginning to savour the news that the Games were coming to London in 2012.

The euphoria was short-lived. Next morning, four terrorists detonated backpack bombs at three Tube stations and on a London bus, claiming the lives of 52 commuters and injuring another 784. Watching the carnage on the TV in my Liverpool office, I counted my lucky stars that I had happened to choose July 6 for our London meeting, and not July 7.

Chapter Seventeen

Our Men in Peshawar

After the shock of the Twin Towers atrocity, I began to settle into my role as editorial director, working with our editors on improving their newspapers and developing their teams. But as I started my second year in the job, the relaunches and training courses were put on the back burner as I was despatched to Pakistan, where one of our reporters had been jailed, accused of being a spy.

My companion on the trip was Charles Collier-Wright, doyen of the Mirror Group Newspapers legal department. On the face of it, Charles and I could hardly be more different. Brought up in Kenya, he has a cut-glass accent and exudes a lawyerly air of unflappable calm. As we took our seats in the first-class section of a Pakistan Airlines Jumbo jet bound for Islamabad, we had several hours to get to know each other. Charles turned out to be wonderful company and we hit it off right away.

We were heading to Pakistan at the behest of Trinity CEO Philip Graf to seek the release of Amardeep Bassey, investigations editor of the Birmingham-based *Sunday Mercury*, who had been arrested on the border with Afghanistan. Amardeep had gone to the region as part of a press trip, arranged by the Foreign Office, to interview British peacekeeping forces but had stayed on to follow up a few additional story ideas. That's when his problems began.

A couple of weeks before departure, his editor David Brookes had come to see me, to seek approval for the side trip. Amardeep had heard that a Western backpacker had been detained in a remote jail near the Pakistan-Afghan border and he wanted to track him down for an interview. If he turned out to be British, it would make a great story. Subject to my agreement, Amardeep would then head for Kabul to interview a British Muslim who was said to be recruiting for the Taliban.

These were not stories a regional paper would normally chase, not least because of the cost, but as he would be out there anyway, and the Foreign Office was paying ...

It wasn't a straightforward decision. This was May 2002, and tensions in the region were high after the American forces' failed attempt to flush Osama Bin Laden from his lair in the Tora Bora caves, in eastern Afghanistan; there was an ongoing humanitarian crisis as tens of thousands of Afghans poured over the border into Pakistan, seeking sanctuary; and there was the small matter of India and Pakistan teetering on the brink of nuclear war.

On the other hand, Amardeep had been to the region previously as a freelance working for the *Sunday Mirror*; he spoke the local languages; he knew the likely risks and knew to take every care. The circumstances that made the place so dangerous also made it compelling territory for a journalist. So, ignoring the small, nagging voice in the back of my head, I gave the go-ahead.

When the official leg of the trip finished, Amardeep recruited two local tribesmen to escort him on his off-piste travels. He found the backpacker, who turned out to be Australian, so the story was of minimal interest in the UK. But when Amardeep and his guides tried to re-enter Pakistan, things quickly went wrong. The border guards noticed he didn't have the correct stamp on his visa, so they arrested him and summoned their superiors, who were immediately suspicious of this Westerner of Indian descent.

As they questioned him, the interrogators' attention turned to his wristwatch – a Christmas gift from his kid brother, purchased at Argos. But it also functioned as a camera, which strengthened their feeling that they had a spy on their hands. They packed him off to a jail in Peshawar, capital of North West Frontier Province, pending further inquiries.

* * * *

The Islamabad Marriott was reputed to be the most heavily-protected hotel in the world*, so the stringent security checks on arrival came as no surprise. What did come as a surprise – and a welcome one – was that the hotel had a small bar, discreetly positioned in the basement, for the use of non-Muslim guests. It was an unexpected oasis where we met a mixture of Brits and Australians, most of them working on engineering projects.

> *The Marriott was a favourite target of terrorists. After a number of foiled attacks, in 2008 an al-Qaeda suicide bomber claimed 54 lives by detonating 600kg of explosives on a truck parked near the hotel.

After checking in, Charles and I arranged to meet a Peshawar-based journalist who doubled up as a fixer, oiling the wheels for Western journalists by using his local knowledge and contacts. He worked for the wonderfully-named *Frontier Post*, a newspaper the government had a penchant for shutting down when the editorial tone offended them.

We also made an appointment to see the British High Commissioner, Sir Hilary Synnott, at his residence on the fortified Western diplomatic compound. Our visitor permits lasted just a week, so if we were going to have any effect, we needed to move quickly.

As a ceiling fan gently stirred the Sunday afternoon air, the High Commissioner gave us tea and a few tips that might come in useful for our trip to Peshawar. He had the manner of a man who had seen the world and could handle anything it threw it him, without breaking sweat. Generously, he put a car, a driver and his assistant consul at our disposal for the journey up country. Trying not to show how jittery I was about visiting a city that had been dubbed "the most dangerous place on Earth", I asked him for the single best piece of advice he could give us. "Don't drink the water," he said.

The next morning, as we set off on the two-hour drive along the Grand Trunk Road, we were advised to lock the doors of the Land Rover Discovery. The journey was notable for two striking sights: the spectacular confluence of the Indus and one of its major tributaries. where a brown tide meets amethyst blue in a roiling, boiling torrent; and the endless human river of black-clad Afghan refugees shuffling silently along the dusty highway, with everything they owned loaded on their backs.

After dropping us off at the Pearl Continental Hotel, our escort headed back to Islamabad. A couple of years earlier, the hotel had been the base for Western journalists covering the Afghan War. Demand for rooms had been so great that they were fully booked for months, with the overspill sleeping on the floor of the foyer, for a fee.

The Pearl had done so well from room charges and the takings from the small, top-floor bar, that a new wing was being built. The only sign that construction was in progress was a solitary workman sitting on the grass in front of the hotel, using a hand saw to cut a long piece of metal. At the speed he was working, the grand opening of the new wing was obviously some way off.

Our fixer said he would set up a meeting for us with a well-connected local lawyer. He, in turn, might be able to engineer a face-to-face with the Home Secretary for North West Frontier Province, who had the power to order Amardeep's release. This sounded like a good plan but when we asked if we could see the lawyer the next day the fixer said: "No, it's a national holiday and everything shuts down. Maybe Wednesday."

The next morning, Charles and I sat in the foyer discussing how to spend our unexpected day off. He had seen a promotional flyer for helicopter trips to the Hindu Kush mountain range and was very keen on it. In my view, this would inevitably end in either a fireball crash or being shot down by the Taliban, so I politely declined. Charles went for a walk around the hotel grounds and by the time he returned he had come up with Plan B. "I don't know if you've noticed but there's a little sign that says 'Championship Golf Course' …"

For around £40, the professional at the Pakistan Air Force Golf Club kitted us out with two sets of rented clubs, a dozen golf balls, a handful of tees, a couple of bottles of water, two baseball caps and a caddy apiece. Around midday, with the temperature nudging 120 degrees Fahrenheit, we set off for 18 holes. Not surprisingly, we were the only players on the course.

Four baking-hot hours later, after an enjoyable but distinctly average round, we sat on the verandah and gulped down bottles of 7Up. We ordered the same again but this time the white-jacketed waiter served us glasses of iced, home-made lemonade. What had the High Commissioner said? Oh yes, don't drink the water. But Charles had picked up his glass and was knocking it back without a care. Was I going to be a sobersides and ask the waiter to take it back? What the heck. Actually, it was delicious. Around three o'clock the next morning I began to pay the price.

* * * *

Next evening, our fixer drove us to a meeting with the lawyer. His office was surrounded by low-rise flats and as our car pulled up several curious children peered down at us from the landings. Then a number of adults emerged. It was obvious that Western faces were a rare sight in these parts.

Sporting a stupendous moustache and a mane of swept-back, silver-grey hair, the lawyer listened to our story. He sat quietly for a moment before holding forth in a booming baritone, punctuated by an occasional theatrical silence. He was careful not to build up our hopes but as we drove back to the hotel, the fixer said he thought the meeting had gone well.

A day and a half later, we were taken to a government building for an audience with the Home Secretary. We were ushered into an office the size of a dance hall, with a huge desk at one end, where the minister was signing documents which were being handed to him ceremonially, one by one, by a poker-faced assistant, who motioned curtly for us to sit down.

The minister, a formidable man in full military uniform, didn't look up. He spent the next few minutes studiously examining his papers and signing them slowly, with great care. We sat silently, waiting. Without uttering a word, he had made it crystal clear where the power in the room lay.

Our fixer had advised us to show due deference and to make our case concisely; the minister was a busy man. We said our piece, appealing for Amardeep's release and asking for permission to see him. The Home Secretary told us he would be subject to due process. When Charles asked if the process could be speeded up, he replied abruptly: "This is fast track!" With that, we understood not to push it any further. We left his office not knowing whether our intervention had made a difference but were told later we would be allowed to make the prison visit.

We met Amardeep in a cordoned-off area not far inside the prison perimeter. He was wearing a dirty, cream-coloured shalwar kameez, and looked shaken and gaunt. He revealed later that another prisoner had threatened to kill him if he refused to convert to Islam. With several guards and prisoners within earshot, we chose our words carefully.

Amardeep told us his two Afghan guides were in jail with him and were helping him get through his ordeal. They hadn't been arrested but had insisted on accompanying him. We asked if there was anything he needed, and he requested a packet of cigarettes, which our fixer quickly rustled up. As he smoked, I noticed his hands were trembling.

The next day, we headed back to Islamabad in an ancient Toyota taxi. It was stiflingly hot, there was no air conditioning and I was still feeling the effects of the golf club lemonade. Hunched in the foetal position in the back of the car, I was desperate to get back to the cool and quiet of my hotel room. Charles, however, had other ideas.

He asked the driver to pull over so he could take a few snaps of a medieval fort he had spotted on our drive up to Peshawar. His "few snaps" turned into a full-blown photo-shoot as he sought out the best angles, tinkered with the shutter speed and ensured the light was just right.

As he crossed the road, attracting the attention of a group of armed policemen, a few thoughts ran through my head: Was the fort still in use as an official building? If so, how might the police react to some Westerner firing off photos like a demented David Bailey? Might we, possibly, be about to join Amardeep in prison? At long, long last, with enough pictures to fill a dozen family albums, Charles got back into the car and we resumed our journey.

Any thought of staying in Pakistan for more than a week was scotched when we were told our visas couldn't be renewed in time. And if we remained without a valid visa, we too risked being arrested. A day later, we were back in the first-class seats, heading home. Although we had been given a hint that he might be released "fairly soon", Amardeep was still languishing in his cell.

Returning to the office, we weren't expecting a hero's welcome, and we didn't get one. The talk was not of our brave bid to have our incarcerated colleague released but of the two of us gallivanting half-way round the world, on company time and expenses, for a round of golf. We had been back a week when we got the news we'd all been hoping for – after 28 days held captive, Amardeep had been released.

Six years later, Amardeep returned to Afghanistan to make a documentary about his experience. He was reunited with the two tribesmen, Noushad Afridi and Khittabshah Shinwari, without whose protection he believes he would have "crumbled". Their tribal customs demanded that they should be prepared to give up their life for a visitor in their care. So they had spent a month in jail, by choice, to ensure the safety of a foreigner they had known for just 48 hours. They are the heroes of this story.

Chapter Eighteen

Facebook, Fake News and the Future

M y generation of Baby Boomer journalists has seen the best of times and the worst of times, as we lived through the most tumultuous period of change in the history of the printed press.

We witnessed the death of the hot metal dinosaur and were present at the birth of computerised publishing. More recently, we have ridden the constant shockwaves of the digital revolution and watched in helpless horror as our advertising lifeblood was leeched away.

Whether with enthusiasm or a sense of trepidation, most journalists have adapted to the new world. Some couldn't, some wouldn't. And several thousand paid the price of change with their jobs. It has been a rocky, challenging ride.

As I hope the preceding pages illustrate, journalism has given me enough fun to fill a working lifetime. That said, the battering the news industry and journalists have taken since the beginning of the 21st Century has been no laughing matter.

The press's struggle for survival in the digital age has been well documented, so I won't dwell on it at length here. But, as the final third of my professional life was spent wrestling this alligator, I'll address some of the issues I faced, and tackle a few widely-held misconceptions.

In the early Noughties, after one false dawn, the Internet started to have a profound and irreversible impact on news publishing's business model. The classified advertising that had been the bedrock of the regional press started to leak away to Rightmove, Auto Trader and a variety of jobs boards. Soon the leak became a dam-burst. In just five years, one of the big regional publishers saw their annual revenue from recruitment advertising alone crash by £100 million. But that was just the *hors d'ouevre*.

In the decade that followed, the tech giants emerged as the dominant publishing platforms – built to a significant extent on content created and paid for by news organisations. They also scooped up swathes of advertising revenue, gutting the news industry commercially.

There's an argument that says traditional media had it coming. According to our critics, we were lazy incumbents who failed to adapt. We gave away our content when we should have charged for it. We were interested only in racking up profits at obscene rates of return. We cut jobs when we should have been investing in journalism. Some of these criticisms are justified. Others, in my opinion, don't hold water.

Profit margins in excess of 30 per cent were not sustainable at a time when the Internet had begun to shake the industry's foundations, but it didn't stop some publishers striving to push them ever upwards. For some, it became a test of their virility to see how high they could go, with little thought for the consequences. And, undeniably, companies should have reinvested more of their profits, years sooner, in the digital future.

But, in my view, the often-repeated accusation that publishers made a fatal mistake by failing to charge for content from the outset does not bear scrutiny. The BBC is ubiquitous, well-funded (enormously so, when compared with commercial news publishers) and well-established in local markets, via local radio and the behemoth bbc.co.uk web site, with its local break-out sections. The BBC invested heavily and cleverly in the web from a very early stage, using their TV and radio strength to promote their burgeoning digital service relentlessly. And they haven't stopped.

The result is a service which is in many ways excellent, but which has encroached unfairly on local media ecosystems, distorting the commercial landscape, limiting the business models available to publishers and, indirectly, reducing the commercial revenue pot.

At the local level, bbc.co.uk's content lacks the depth of most commercially-funded publishers, but it has one magic ingredient – it is free. In readers' eyes, that makes it an oven-ready, good-enough substitute, should local newspapers attempt to charge for their content.

Regional publishers have flirted with paywalls for years. Every time, the experiment was swiftly curtailed as they saw their digital audience crash by around 90 per cent, almost overnight.

In the early days of the Internet, there was a saying that: "The only things that make money on the web are the Three Fs – football, finance and … pornography." These days, I'm not so sure about football. In my view, paywalls never were and never will be the saviour of the regional press – or, for that matter, the national tabloids, which compete fiercely over a very similar mix of content, principally entertainment news, celebrity gossip and sport. So long as one of them remains free-to-air, so must the others.

At the top end of the market, the *Wall Street Journal* and the *Financial Times* have had success with paywalls, not because of their news content but because the unique financial data they provide is a must-have for businesses. The other "posh" papers – *The Times*, *The Guardian* and the *Daily Telegraph* – have, each in their different ways, built respectable subscription-based audiences.

In a highly-uncertain market, one thing seems clear – there is no one-size-fits-all solution to the conundrum of finding a sustainable publishing model. The answer for the tabloids and the regionals is more likely to lie in a much wider mixture of revenue sources than the traditional combination of advertising and cover price which sustained print for so long.

The Internet-driven revenue crash was so severe that job cuts were unavoidable. Over the course of 16 years as editorial director of Reach plc's regional titles, I was responsible for leading more than 40 cost-saving restructures, as a consequence of which many journalism roles were lost. Journalists were not the only ones to suffer; colleagues in advertising, newspaper sales and all the back-of-house departments have also felt a great deal of pain.

It used to be a truism among newspaper finance directors that the industry's two biggest costs were people and paper, so these were the main ports of call when major cost savings were required. But cutting either of them comes at a price.

Lower pagination means less value for money for the reader, which inevitably causes some to stop buying. Raising the price of the newspaper can help to fill the revenue gap but that triggers a further loss of readers. It's a brutally simple equation – the bigger the price increase, the more readers you will lose.

At the current, mature stage of printed newspapers' life cycle, circulations and paginations are a fraction of the glory days, which means paper is no longer the major cost-reduction lever it used to be. So the focus falls on people.

You can usually get away with reducing the number of journalists on your books, in the short term at least. Journalists, in the main, are driven by a love of what they do and a commitment to producing a quality product. They will go the extra mile, put in the extra hours, cover for the lost jobs.

But eventually, after multiple rounds of downsizing, something has to give. That something is breadth and depth of coverage. When big stories break, newsrooms still react, often magnificently. But the everyday coverage – court and council reporting, and the workaday local stories that fill the middle of the paper – has become thinner. Less resource also means less time to plan and to be creative, forcing newsrooms to be more reactive and products to become that little bit more bland.

A single, well-executed cost-saving restructure may go almost unnoticed by the reader. But as the revenue continued to drain away, cost saving became an ongoing necessity. You can't defy gravity forever – eventually, editorial quality suffers. Society pays a price too, as the press's ability to fulfil its role as public watchdog is eroded.

It's not only the products that feel the pressure. In the era of fake news, "alternative facts" and social media trolling, life as a journalist has become significantly tougher. Faced with an ocean of content, it is difficult for readers to sort fact from fiction, with the result that some no longer trust anything they read, whatever the source.

At the street level, reporters across the UK regularly face abuse, threats and even physical attacks as they go about their job of bringing the news of the day to the communities they serve. Young, female reporters are a particular target. It's an ugly state of affairs.

Despite all these difficulties, editors and their teams are constantly conjuring up initiatives to help bridge the resource gap and rising to the challenge of building a digital audience big enough and loyal enough to sustain the business in the long term.

The goal I set myself at Reach was to find the new business model for regional titles, which I believe must be based on editorial departments being profitable in their own right. I gave it my all but when I left the company, on December 31, 2017, the new model had eluded me; digital revenue growth had failed to match the boom in audiences, and stand-alone editorial profitability was still some way off.

But since then, a number of hopeful signs have emerged. The online audience for regional content has continued to grow, and now typically accounts for around 90 per cent of the total, with just ten per cent coming from print. The readers who slowly but steadily deserted newspapers have been replaced, with interest, by a new generation who never buy a paper but are voracious consumers of information via their smartphones.

Many titles have more readers now than when I began my career in 1974, and those readers have a strong interest in news, sport and what's on in their local area – the meat and drink of regional publishing. It seems to me that the path to a sustainable future lies in understanding these growing audiences, engaging with them to cement their loyalty and using their personal data judiciously to provide editorial and commercial services they value and trust.

The Covid pandemic brought its own, particular challenges but the news media responded magnificently, switching from office-based to home working in a matter of days, with barely a blip, and without the reader noticing. It was a great achievement which showed that, when they have to, publishing businesses can move mountains.

Covid has also given regional publishing an unexpected shot in the arm. Newspaper sales were hit during lockdown – although not as severely as some had feared – because people chose to stay safe in their homes rather than venture out to the newsagent's. But online audiences boomed as readers turned to their local title's digital channels for the most reliable, up-to-date news on how the pandemic was affecting their part of the world. And revenue has followed, as advertisers realised the most effective way to reach these significant audiences is – just like the old days – via the local news publisher.

There are also signs the tech giants have accepted – late in the day and grudgingly – that they are not just platforms but publishers, with all the implications that has for governance, proper content management and a duty of care to users. There are signs, too, of a fairer commercial deal emerging for the news media, whose content has helped the giants achieve their position of global super-dominance.

Most encouraging of all, regional publishers are launching new web sites and have begun recruiting again, as they pin their strategy – and the future of their business – on their relevance to local communities, based on high-quality, digitally-led content.

As a young reporter, all I had to worry about was taking a good shorthand note, writing my story and hitting the edition deadline. Today's journalist writes stories, takes photographs, shoots and edits video, creates social media posts, hosts and produces podcasts, understands search engine optimisation and can use digital analytics programs to drive audience growth and engagement with readers.

They produce far more content than my generation ever did, across an array of media platforms. They are smart, highly skilled, prolific, endlessly adaptable, quick to learn and remarkably resilient.

They are the torch bearers for the future of UK journalism. I take my hat off to them and wish them every success. And as they make their way in the industry I love, I hope they have more than their fair share of fun.

ACKNOWLEDGEMENTS

Heartfelt thanks for their help and encouragement to my friends and colleagues Charles Collier-Wright, Debbie Coxon, Jenny Gibson, David Gledhill, Mike Glover, Jonathan Grun, Ian Lyness, Tony Hill, Gerry Hunt, Neil Jagger, Barrie Jones, Dave Morton and Paul New.

Thank you to my publisher Steven Hodder, to my children for their invaluable input, and to my wife Jo for her editing skill.

BIBLIOGRAPHY

The Pottery Cottage Murders, by Carol Ann Lee and Peter Howse

The Municipal Dreams blog

The Blackpool Crime blog

Bob Cummings and The Daily Drone web site

The Horny Handed Subs of Toil Facebook group

Mike Dempsey's blog

Lightning Source UK Ltd.
Milton Keynes UK
UKHW021930310122
397988UK00007B/1664